God's Mighty Acts Around the Globe

Including a

Study Discussion Guide with Questions and Activities

Robert B. Watkins

Robert B. Watkins

All scripture quotations, except where noted, are taken from the Holy Bible, NEW INTERNATIONAL VERSION®. Copyright © 1973, 1978, 1984, 2011 by Biblica, Inc. All rights reserved worldwide. Used by permission.

Production rights for the cover photo were purchased royalty free from vasakkohaline@Dreamstime.com. Author's photo on the back cover is used with the permission of Tim Steffen.

Copyright © 2014 Robert B. Watkins

All rights reserved.

ISBN-10: 1497537975
ISBN-13: 978-1497537972

DEDICATION

I dedicate this book to Marji, my wife. Her love, vitality, good humor, and faithfulness have provided the foundation for our life of joy and excitement. With considerable sacrifice in terms of our time together, she has granted me the freedom to follow my passion for global missions. I could not have chased my dreams and done my job without her support and encouragement.

Robert B. Watkins

ACKNOWLEDGEMENTS

I thank the membership of the Cumberland Presbyterian Church for supporting my ministry for more than forty-five years as a minister, missionary, and mission executive.

Enough good things cannot be said about the missionaries with whom I have worked. These men and women labor daily as evangelists, humanitarians, social workers, teachers, preachers, encouragers, and a host of other responsibilities. The world is a better place because of their faithfulness and sacrifice.

I also owe a great debt to the many international friends who have received me in their homes and countries as a brother in Christ. Their hospitality and love for the global nature of the church never ceases to amaze me.

The staff, past and present, of the Mission Ministry Team and the Ministry Council of the Cumberland Presbyterian Church has taught me the meaning of unity, mutual acceptance, and unselfish service.

Along with my wife, Margie Shannon, Jinger Ellis, Margie Barger Vanderlaan, Martha Mims, and Chet and Diane Dickson have provided significant assistance in reviewing the material for this book, as well as other submissions in recent years. I owe a great debt to Cindy Hoffner Martin for doing the final editing of this book.

Finally, I owe a priceless debt to Rev. Joe Matlock. He recruited me for the position of the Director of Global Missions of the Cumberland Presbyterian Church. And, that opportunity led to a fulfilling life of service in global ministry.

Table of Contents

DEDICATION iii

ACKNOWLEDGEMENTS iv

INTRODUCTION ix
U.S.A. 1993 ix
   "A Musical Gift to Remember" ix

SECTION 1 1
God's Mighty Acts Around the Globe 1
Costa Rica 1975 11
   "Joy to the World, Friends Have Come" 11
Costa Rica 1975 13
   "Metaphorically Speaking" 13
Colombia 1976 15
   "The Sharing of a Special Meal" 15
Colombia 1976 18
   "A Taxi Driver Becomes the Good Samaritan" 18
Colombia 1976 22
   "Another Missionary Christmas Story" 22
Colombia 1977 24
   "Mi Familia Me Botó" 24
   "Hot Air Balloons on a Bus" 26
Colombia 1978 32
   "The Day Jaime Decided to Become a Missionary" ... 32
No Particular Place—Any Specific Time 36
   "The Society for the Picking of Apples" 36
Colombia 1978 39
   "Not Going to the Dogs" 39
U.S.A. 1979 44
   "Emmaus Road Experience" 44
U.S.A. 1980 45
   "The Child's Mite" 45
U.S.A. 1980 46
   "The Conversion of a Dump" 46
China 1980 47

"Where Should We Evangelize?" 47
U.S.A. 1980 .... **48**
"Could Prayer Be the Only Answer?" 48
Colombia 1982 .... **50**
"Should I or Shouldn't I?" 50
Colombia 1983 .... **53**
"The Eye of the Tiger" 53
Ecuador 1983 .... **56**
"The Pitfalls of Prosperity" 56
U.S.A. 1990 .... **57**
"Respecting the Seventh Generation" 57
Colombia 1991—2013 .... **58**
"The Power of Unity within the Body of the Church" 58
China 1991 .... **61**
"The Impossible Made Tangible" 61
Africa 1991 .... **63**
"Just Getting There and Home Is a Mission in Itself" 63
China 1991 .... **68**
"Blood-Stained Glory" 68
U.S.A. 1993 .... **71**
"A Mission Challenge" 71
Macau 1993 .... **74**
"The Gift of Hospitality" 74
Japan 1995 .... **77**
"Giving Back" 77
Russian Republics 1995 .... **77**
"Using the Cultural Decorum for Faith Purposes" 77
Colombia 2000 .... **79**
"God Spoke Very Loudly Here" 79
Colombia 2000 .... **82**
"A Friend Sent Me" 82
Brazil 2004 .... **83**
"On a Rock in a Hard Spot" 83
Myanmar 2004 .... **86**
"On the Roads of Mandalay" 86
Dominican Republic 2005 .... **89**
"The Least People of the World" 89

U.S.A. 2005	**91**
"Recognizing God's Involvement in Your Life"	91
Mongolia 2006	**92**
"Giving Away What You Would Like to Keep!"	92
Mongolia 2006	**95**
"Where Two or Three Gather"	95
South Korea and Afghanistan 2008	**97**
"How Will God Work Out This Tragedy?"	97
Central Asia 2009	**100**
"Door #1, Door #2, or Door #3"	100
U.S.A. 2009	**101**
"It's Amazing Who Celebrates Christmas"	101
Israel 2012	**102**
"A Quiet Dove"	102
Tanzania 2013	**105**
"The News We Prefer to Ignore"	105
U.S.A. 2013	**106**
"Opening and Closing Your Heart"	106
SECTION 2	**109**
Spiritual Stories as a Form of Witness	**109**
Hints about Writing and Telling the Story	**109**
NOTES	**119**
A Study Guide	121
Introduction	121
ABOUT THE AUTHOR	**172**

Robert B. Watkins

INTRODUCTION

No other form of witness penetrates the heart as profoundly as a STORY!

U.S.A. 1993

"A Musical Gift to Remember"

"Saul's attendants said to him, 'See, an evil spirit from God is tormenting you. Let our lord command his servants here to search for someone who can play the lyre. He will play when the evil spirit from God comes on you, and you will feel better.' Whenever the spirit from God came on Saul, David would take up his lyre and play. Then relief would come to Saul; he would feel better, and the evil spirit would leave him" (1 Samuel 16:15, 16, 23).

Rev. Arturo Taborda visited the United States in 1993 for a denominational meeting in Little Rock, Arkansas. Simultaneously, the Women's Convention of the same denomination met in the same city. Rev. Taborda and three Colombian women had been invited to share their testimonies with the attendees of the convention. While the women were willing to speak, Rev. Taborda, a quiet saintly gentleman, preferred to play two selections on his violin. He had played the instrument by ear since childhood.

The women took turns articulating their personal experiences with Christ, when they finished; the silver-headed Rev. Taborda tenderly carried his violin onto the stage. He smiled cautiously and said in broken English, "I play Mozart and a hymn." His brief presentation would be the last event of the morning's activities. And, it would set in motion a life changing experience.

Rev. Arturo had reached the age when his thick curly hair was totally silver and always combed in a natural flow from the front to the back without a part. His brazen eyebrows gleamed in the stage light. It was not his custom to smile as he played, but instead his personality seemed to disappear into a focus of concentration on the music he had chosen. It was as if his mind and spirit disappeared into the violin and then reappeared in the form of harmonic sounds.

His performance created intense emotion as all eyes were fixed upon the violin of this pastor from one of the poorest barrios of Medellin, Colombia, an area called Zamora. This dangerous district was once the home of many of the henchmen of then drug lord, Pablo Escobar. No doubt some of the drug vendors had heard of the ministry of Rev. Taborda and his effort to help people escape from the dangers of the drug culture.

Following the presentation, the Colombians and I were some of the first to exit the conference hall. We stood in a large display area available for conversation and questions. I observed the attendees as they left, hoping to capture a visual sense of the impact of the presentations.

Most of the conferees had left when I noticed a middle-aged woman coming toward us. She caught my attention because she looked like someone leaving a rodeo arena. She wore tight, faded blue denims, a western-patterned shirt, and beaded unpolished cowboy boots. She was a contemporary cowgirl ready for a day of riding on the ranch, except for spurs and a beaver-skin hat. She walked slowly with a stiffness that testified to a few years in the saddle. It soon became apparent that the woman was crying. Tears were falling with enough frequency that she had a tissue and was blotting them as she walked up. Dabbing at her eyes, she said, "Dr. Watkins, would you please translate and tell Rev. Taborda what just happened to me during his presentation?" She said, "When I came to the service today, my heart was not in it. A little over a year ago my father died after a long bout with cancer, and I have not been able to get over my loss and grief. I have been depressed and nearly unable to function as a wife or a mother. But, today, when Arturo took the stage, something incredible happened. My father played the violin. And, when Arturo began to play Gaither's 'Because He Lives, I Can Face Tomorrow,' I recalled that was Dad's favorite hymn."

She paused, but not to wipe her tears; instead, for the first time since she approached, she smiled ever so faintly. "As Arturo played, it was as if I felt the Holy Spirit descend, rest upon my shoulders, and then depart with the burden of my grief! Oh, I am still crying, but now the pain has been replaced with a certainty of hope and thanksgiving. I just wanted to say thanks," she continued.

We paused and prayed. Then she was gone, carrying the quiet gift of Don Arturo, a man who could not speak English, but whose violin was the instrument to heal a broken heart.

Robert B. Watkins

SECTION 1

God's Mighty Acts Around the Globe

God's presence in the world constantly amazes us. We are intrigued by God's desire to interact with us. As a holy parent, interest in a child is natural and profound. We wonder how much of God's interest in and interaction with us we can identify. Since God is omnipresent, how many times does God's Spirit sweep in, around, and through us with or without our notice? Many questions flood our minds. People have asked similar questions since the beginning of time. The psalmist pondered the relationship between God and humans. "What is mankind that you are mindful of them, human beings that you care for them?" (Psalm 8:4). "Where can I go from your Spirit? Where can I flee from your presence? If I go up to the heavens, you are there; if I make my bed in the depths, you are there. If I rise on the wings of the dawn, if I settle on the far side of the sea, even there your hand will guide me, your right hand will hold me fast" (Psalm 139:7-10).

God wants to relate with us. God listens. God speaks. God influences our daily lives. God calls. The Bible is mainly one story after another of God's interaction with men and women, and the impact of those relationships upon history. What makes it possible to identify the touch of God in our lives? At some point in our spiritual maturation we are given the spiritual perception that allows us to recognize God's desire to love us. The key is training our perception to see and recognize such special experiences.

If we believe in a personal God, we should expect a potential surprise from God at any moment. Once we learn to "know" the Lord and listen for his interaction in our life, we are compelled to share this marvelous relationship in the best ways possible to reveal the personal nature of God to people who have not recognized it. Spiritual storytelling is one of the best tools to communicate the beauty of this supernatural dimension of life.

The story of Eli and Samuel in 1 Samuel 3 presents in a simple way one of the most important lessons every child or adult should learn in his/her pilgrimage through life. The lesson is clear—"God speaks to you and God yearns that you will pay attention and respond!"

Here's the story. Many years ago, long before Jesus was born, a young Jewish woman named Hannah was distraught because she could not have a baby. She eventually pleaded her case with God through prayer, promising that if God would give her a son, she would give him to the Lord. Some would question such a bargain. Why birth a son if you can't even raise him? Others might make the promise and then not follow through with the verbal commitment, but not Hannah!

God honored her persistent prayers and gave her a son whom she named Samuel. As promised, after he was weaned, she took him to the temple at Shiloh and left him under the care of the priest, Eli. The boy served faithfully in the temple until he reached the age when he had the capacity of mind and conscience to think and act on his own volition.

During the dark of night, Samuel heard his name called, "SAMUEL." Samuel ran to Eli's room and said, "Here I am." Eli told Samuel that he had not called him and sent him back to bed. Samuel heard his name a second time and ran to Eli's room, but Eli again sent him back to bed.

At this point in the Bible story, the writer added, "Now Samuel did not yet know the Lord: The word of the Lord had not yet been revealed to him" (I Samuel 3:7). This story is one of the few places in the Bible where we see a clear example of what we call "reaching the age of accountability." It is an amazing report of a universal rite of passage. At some point and some age God initiates a relationship with us—the divine God speaks to the emerging adult that has matured sufficiently mentally, emotionally and spiritually to understand the impact of relating to his or her Creator.

The boy heard the call of his name the third time and rushed to Eli's bedside. This time Eli realized the spiritual transformation that was occurring in young Samuel. So, Eli sent Samuel back to bed with some important instructions. When you hear your name called the next time, say, "Speak, Lord, your servant is listening."

Actually Eli served as a language interpreter. He helped Samuel to distinguish between a human and a divine conversation. New believers often have to be taught to hear and respond to God's voice in their lives. And, Eli, despite his inability to discipline his own adolescent/young adult children, did a splendid job of opening Samuel's door into listening and responding to God's touch upon his life. Samuel's response to the voice of God was the beginning of a life-long relationship between God and Samuel.

Three of life's greatest blessings are spirituality, humor, and memories. Spirituality allows people to explore the relationship between the Creator and the created. Humor reminds us not to take life too seriously, moving most sadness at least temporarily to a smile. Memories transport us in an instant to our past to review those experiences the mind recorded as significant.

This book primarily records my experiences with the powerful presence of God as witnessed around the globe. The first part of the book follows a chronology to weave humor and inspiration into one fabric, just as they appear in everyone's life. Additionally, I have incorporated a limited number of stories provided by other writers.

This book will illustrate time and again that God pursues a similar relationship with every person on earth. It records contemporary stories similar to Samuel's. The stories recount experiences I have observed that demonstrate God's active pursuit of people in order to guide, love, encourage and protect them. Ultimately, God's love for humans impresses us with a quality in a divine being we find in no other religion. Our God is a personal God. Our God pursues his children the same way a shepherd cares for every lamb in the flock. The beauty and impact of that intimacy between humankind and God ultimately brings glory to God.

The inspirational stories intend to give glory to God for God's loving personal nature. The ultimate purpose of all we do should be aimed to move the focus to the glory of God. The first question of the greater catechism of the Presbyterian tradition reads: "What is the chief end of man? The chief end of man is to glorify God and enjoy Him forever." Some people substitute "love of God" for the "glory of God." The two terms are really not the same. The love of God is one element of the glory of God. Giving glory to God really means witnessing to the reality of God's presence in the world. It is our witness that God is around us and we have seen God.

The following stories also attempt to provoke a desire within the heart of the reader to recall and record his or her own stories of God's mighty acts in their own lives. Erin Morgenstern in *The Night Circus* writes: "You may tell a tale that takes up residence in someone's soul, becomes their blood and self and purpose. That tale will move them and drive them and who knows what they might do because of it, because of your words. That is your role, your gift."[1] As

Matthew wrote: "Let your light shine to glorify your father in heaven" (Matthew 5:16). Your stories, similar to those in this book, will record your pilgrimage with a God so interested in forming a relationship with you that God does amazing acts in your life.

Following these stories, you will be given brief direction in story writing and storytelling so you can also witness to God's mighty acts. Hopefully, you will want to write some of your stories in an effort to testify to your family and the world that you are privileged to know God. Your story is a "love story" about God's love for you. It deserves to be written.

But for now enjoy reading about the God whom many call "friend."

I grew up on a farm in southeastern Iowa. Life in the 1950s for a tenant farmer was tedious financially; however, my parents planned ahead for my college education. They purchased two ewes and borrowed a ram for me to start a herd of sheep. My flock had grown to nearly forty sheep by the time I was a junior in high school and I was winning top prizes at the annual county fair with frequency. Then tragedy struck.

One evening, I forgot to lock my sheep in the protection of the barn. I woke up with a start and immediately thought of the flock. I ran through the back lot and down the dirt driveway past our two ponds filled with fish and bullfrogs to the hillside where the sheep normally grazed, but they were not there. By then, panic drove my legs faster and faster as I scanned the hillsides from field to field. My horrid fear was confirmed as I spotted my fallen charge. The wild dogs had left eight dead, ten brutally torn and gashed; and, those unharmed physically were still trembling from the assault. I stood and cried over my flock. It was a nightmare that had actually happened. I learned the real consequences for sheep left without a shepherd. A script to help the defenseless and weak was being written in my heart. I didn't realize its impact at the time, but God deeply etched this experience into the core of my being.

As I think about the people of the world today, my heart fills with compassion. Many, like those sheep, are spiritually dead without a faith in a higher being. Others are brutally torn by the world, unable to find a sense of security. Many of the masses live in fear with no answer for their anxiety. They wait and watch expectantly for some witness of resolve or hope.

This painful experience was likely one of the first times I felt the birth of a motivation and purpose that would eventually feed my energy and fulfillment. God used this horrible experience as a foundation stone for what would become my life's work and passion. I consider this a pivotal moment in my life, even though I didn't fully recognize it at the time. Even today, I periodically revisit those pastures in my mind's eye to refresh my zeal for a life of service.

Life is formed by a composite of experiences that build one upon the other. Most of those experiences are so subtle that we are unable to identify them or their impact upon our life. However, there are other more pivotal experiences that carry the possibility of initiating a 180-degree shift in what we will do and who we will become. Such shifts occur infrequently, but they are undeniable and usually identifiable.

I can identify small influences that changed my world view, helped me focus on what was and was not important, taught me right from wrong, and led to my understanding of talents and spiritual gifts.

We understand why we are the way we are when we retrace our life to identify such transformational moments and how we responded to them. It is like walking backwards with a personal characteristic in hand trying to find the place or moment where we picked it up. Transitional moments can be negative experiences such as the premature loss of a parent that drove us into a responsibility for our family that we certainly didn't want or expect. Or, on the positive side, they can be the special attention given by a teacher that birthed our positive self-concept. Every moment carries the potential for a positive or negative impact upon life, but only a few really make dramatic and immediate changes.

The history of Saul in the Book of Acts, chapter 9, illustrates a pivotal moment that radically changed not only his life, but affected the future of the world. You may recall that Paul had been a major figure in the arrest and persecution of Christians in the months immediately after the death of Jesus. One day his attitude and purpose changed radically during a trip from Jerusalem to Damascus where he intended to identify and arrest a group of Christians. While walking with friends, he was blinded by a bright light, reprimanded by Jesus, and instructed to go to Damascus and await further instructions. He remained blind for three days. The experience climaxed with God sending a believer named Ananias to visit Saul. Ananias healed him from blindness and Saul was filled with the Holy Spirit. In a matter of hours, Saul became a promoter rather than an opponent of the birth of a new faith. He began to preach immediately his belief that Jesus was the Messiah. These were the first steps toward his becoming the greatest theologian of the New Testament. This personal encounter with God was just one of the uncountable billions that would take place over the next two thousand years. I have had several such encounters with the ever-present Holy Spirit. One such experience occurred after three years in my first full-time pastorate.

I attended a meeting of our denomination in Savannah, Tennessee in the early months of 1974. These meetings were generally scripted to affirm specific recommendations made by the various committees and presented to the larger body for a vote. Since most decisions were cut and dried, the meetings appeared largely a waste of time.

This was an event I might have considered skipping if I could have found an acceptable excuse.

The highlight of such a business meeting usually took place in the form of "koinonia" (fellowship) over lunch. And, on a good day, participants heard a good sermon and inspiring music.

I settled into my pew for worship hoping we could finish worship and business during the morning, thus allowing me time to rush home for the Vanderbilt basketball game. I had no idea that God had another incredible and unbelievable plan in mind. Rev. Buddy Stott, a missionary to Japan, was the guest speaker for the morning worship service. I had heard of this fellow because he was one of the few missionaries in our denomination and his service was often highlighted in denominational publications.

He appeared a very humble man with little pretense. His small stature, his simple black suit and narrow black tie sent the advance expectation that something conservative was about to occur. His steps to the pulpit were short and measured, marked with an expected missionary piety. I felt that some of the reserve of the Japanese culture had rubbed off on him. But, from the beginning, his quiet gentle demeanor mesmerized me. His sermon became spellbinding when he began to speak of the commitment of Christians in the face of persecution. He spoke of incidents when believers were buried up to their necks under the sand of the beach. They were given the opportunity to repent of their faith or await certain death when the tide rose later in the day. He was noticeably touched as he said, "All of those buried were martyred."

I do not recall him challenging the congregation to give consideration to a career in missions or encouraging the people to make a financial contribution. Truth be known, I had never been interested in missions, nor had I tried to motivate my congregation to strengthen its missions program. So I was surprised he was able to keep my attention. But, in one of the most significant pivotal moments in my brief life, I felt a silent voice calling me to do whatever necessary to become a missionary. It was just that simple. I had no idea what the new revelation implied; it was just there. I was certain. God touched the depth of something within me with this new challenge.

My first response was a period of confusion and reflection. What could this mean? As I tried to sort it out, I became more and more uncomfortable with the idea. I wished God had addressed this personal message to another recipient. I was as happy in my work as I could have hoped. Our church membership was growing quantitatively and qualitatively. Mostly, I was happy with the young couples joining our church and growing in their commitment to Christ as well. My job was usually fun and exciting. I learned something new everyday. This missionary concern was so unbelievable and unwanted that I couldn't bring myself to share the experience with my wife. So, I didn't. On the exterior I moved ahead with life as usual, trying to forget the "feeling" I had experienced in Savannah. Fortunately, God chose not to be ignored.

In June of 1974, just a few months after my Savannah moment, my wife and I traveled to another denominational meeting. Virginia followed Rev. John Lovelace into a buffet line for lunch. They chatted as they moved through the line and John said, "You know, you and Bob should give some thought and prayer to becoming missionaries. John's words penetrated to that deep point where spiritual decisions are considered and made. And, she took notice! But like myself, she remained silent about the unwelcome thought. We didn't know it, but the lasso thrown around us would only be pulled tighter and tighter over the next few months.

In November we traveled to Iowa to visit my parents. During the return trip, I became overwhelmed with the power of God's calling upon my life. I said, "Virginia, I need to share a spiritual dilemma I am facing." She said, "Before you talk about that, let me tell you about a struggle I am facing." Our sharing of very similar callings united us in a way we had not experienced before. There was no doubt that God had a plan that required the full commitment of both of us. But, we confessed to each other that we really didn't want to make such a shift in our short-term plan for our life. Our first child had been born in August and it seemed so unreal to consider uprooting our family to go into mission work. Nor, did we have any idea of how to pursue such a calling. The when, where, and how to respond to God's initiative remained unanswered.

So, we put the idea on simmer and didn't mention the possibility during December or the early days of January. Then, the January edition of our denominational magazine arrived in the mail. I opened it to the first page and saw the headline—"The Effort to Recruit a Missionary for Colombia Goes Unanswered." I was at the church office at the time, so I locked the church and drove home to show the article to Virginia. We immediately decided that this was another sign of God's call upon our lives. We decided that enough was enough. There was no reason to continue to fight against the obvious.

The article indicated that anyone interested in this opportunity should call the Board of Missions. We made the call and the Director of World Missions arranged to meet with us the following Wednesday. That meeting resulted in a job offer; three months later we were in San Jose, Costa Rica for a year of Spanish language training. Neither of us could have predicted the wonderful world that would open before our very eyes.

Costa Rica 1975

"Joy to the World, Friends Have Come"

Thanksgiving, 1975, would not be our typical family holiday because we lived in San Jose, Costa Rica. We moved four months prior and the time passed ever so slowly, like the months before I got my first driver's license. I felt I must nudge the hour hand of the clock to force it to cycle twice and signal another passed day. Language learning proved the most difficult task I had undertaken. My mouth wanted to utter a lot of phrases, but I couldn't say them in Spanish. Living in a foreign land forced me to make comparisons between what was and what is. The results were depressing. Whoever wrote absence makes the heart grow fonder was a confused romantic. Absence makes the heart grow resentful. I became more than a bit upset with God for calling us as missionaries to Colombia. What was God thinking? We felt the despair of the present, but had little hope the future would improve.

Had my calling to serve not been so certain, I would have thrown in the towel and returned to the U.S.A. where they eat pumpkin pie on Thanksgiving, where people know the meaning of Pilgrim, and where Thanksgiving signals a hint of winter.

My wife and I had fallen into the same pit of discouragement at the same time, and we began to wonder whether there was an exit. This whole experience was also like a very slippery mountain that tested our faith, determination, and commitment. It wore down even our resistance to illness. I contracted walking pneumonia that stole 30 pounds from my plump body. Where was our family when we needed them? The truth was they didn't want us to leave in the first place, so we had to sleep in the bed we had created for ourselves.

We were lying in bed after a turkey-less Thanksgiving and I said, "If you think this is bad, can you imagine a Christmas away from family and friends?" This statement revealed that Christmas would be lonely, very lonely. Suddenly, reality raised its ugly head and screamed. And, equally bad, we saw none of the normal Christmas signals of late November.

The temperature read 85 °F instead of 30 °F. (29 °C instead of -1 °C) No one peddled Christmas trees in the lot next to the supermarket. Fisher Price toys for tots didn't exist except through the mail and then the recipient could expect delays and taxation at the customs office. This year our closest extended family within a thousand miles would be easy to visit because we all lived in the same house.

Of course, we made new missionary family traditions, but that brought little solace when compared with what we would miss.

Those laments resurfaced daily from Thanksgiving until December 10th when we got a most unexpected phone call from our wonderful church friends, Dr. and Mrs. Robert Bourne from Camden, Tennessee. They always served as our sounding board for both the good and the bad, and always called when we needed them most. Anne started the conversation, "How are things going for you?"

Virginia replied, "We are hanging in here, but there isn't a lot of joy in our house, even though it is nearly Christmas."

Dr. Bob said, "We have a little present that we are sending your way that might help." Visions of a "care package" immediately popped into my head—a fruitcake, a country ham, and some North American toys for David. "It is scheduled to arrive on December 22 at 6:30 p.m. But you will need to pick it up."

I responded, "What do you mean?"

Anne continued, "You will need to go to the Juan Santamaría International Airport and wait in the baggage area until you see Bobby and Elizabeth. We are sending them to brighten your Christmas!" We were speechless. Elizabeth was our son's #1 baby sitter during his first year of life and almost like a daughter to us. They were 18 and 16 and their parents were sending them to spend their Christmas vacation with us.

Such love and sharing still rocks me. Of course it can't compare to God's gift of Jesus to the world. It was not an incarnational experience since only God could send his son to be human and dwell among us, but it was a spiritual demonstration of agape love that remains one of the most precious gifts of my life. It definitely modeled in a concrete way the divine love of God who sent his son to dwell among those he loved. But in a human sense, the gift of two kids for Christmas "saved" us by transforming sadness to joy. That year, we sang "Joy to the World, Some Friends Have Come!"

Costa Rica 1975

"Metaphorically Speaking"

"Should I go or not?" I struggled about whether I should attend a *corrido* de *toros* (bullfight)? My preconception of a bullfight included torture for an innocent animal. Yet, for some reason, I wanted to attend. I had read Hemingway's book, *Death in the Afternoon*, in preparation for living in Latin America. It passionately defended the art form of bullfights.

I thought, "If Hemingway found this so compelling, it must have some value." But then my mind flitted to the perspective of the bull.

Why do people like to watch an animal be driven mad? Finally I justified my attendance under the guise of having a cultural experience.

Bullfights mean *ferias* (colorful carnivals, exciting music, and rowdy crowds). Out of necessity we parked miles from the bullring and fell into step with the masses as they laughed, pushed, and primed their party pumps from a *bota* (wine skin) full of sangria. They drank as they walked, sometimes slobbering or spilling the alcohol down the front of their shirts. It was obvious some folks had started drinking long before leaving home. The ticket booths had lines of fifty to seventy people, so we were glad we had arrived early. Obviously, many people would fail to secure a ticket. Yet, everyone followed the endless lines. Breaking line could result in a fight; the offender would definitely be outnumbered.

According to Hemingway, the quality of a bullfight depends entirely on the bull and the bullfighter. A bull that doesn't charge, and charge, and charge again will not allow the bullfighter to demonstrate the beauty of the sport. As it was, I soon learned we would not see the real thing. The traditional Spanish bullfight had undergone specific changes in Costa Rica that diminished it from what a tourist would have seen in Spain or other Latin American countries. The Costa Ricans no longer allowed the matador to kill the bull after each fight. So the great bullfighters didn't even stop in Costa Rica.

To compensate and draw large crowds, the *Ticos* (Costa Ricans) allowed anyone older than eighteen and sober to fight the bull. The fight often began with a hundred and fifty young screaming men and a couple of women filling the ring, waiting for the bull to break wildly through the entrance gate. When the bull entered, immediately one hundred and forty teens and young adults scrambled wildly over the sides of the ring. From the beginning mob of so-called *toreros*, only ten or fewer were really ready to challenge the bull up close and personal. A few poor slow souls got trampled in the mayhem and others were tossed wildly into the air by the hornless angry bulls, much like bronco riders at a rodeo. As the bull tired from charging the jeering youngsters, it stood confused in the ring trying to catch a breath, when some young man would sneak up from the rear and try to mount the bull, only to land in the dust when the bull began to spin in surprise. Eventually, the bull lost interest and the attendants drove it from the ring. And, it all started again. At the end of the day, hundreds of adventurers claimed the name of "Bullfighter," but only a few deserved it.

As I sat and witnessed the show, I recognized a parable of religious faithfulness. It is one thing to say, "I am a Christian!" It is another thing all together to stay in the ring when placed face-to-face with an enemy of Christianity.

Colombia 1976

"The Sharing of a Special Meal"

What meal would you consider as one of the most significant of your life? And, why would you select that particular meal? Was it a "last supper" with a loved one? Did it seal a deal that greatly increased your wealth? Or, was it the meal when you proposed to the one you loved? For me to share with you one of my special meals, I must give some background related to the pain of "culture shock."

The powerful, debilitating effects of culture shock attack victims in ways that cannot be predicted. It is an individualistic disorientation due to a significant shift in one's way of life, particularly when visiting or moving to another country. Most people never consider culture shock until it affects them.

The symptoms include disorientation, boredom, excessive criticism of the new culture, depression, staring, sleepiness, mood swings, bursts of anger or crying, etc. No prescribed medicine will resolve culture shock. In most cases improvement results through exposure to the new environment, mental/emotional adjustments, and an acceptance of the new culture into one's personality. Most authorities agree that culture shock should improve within the first year of moving to a new country.

Our first struggle with culture shock struck to some degree during our transitional year after moving from the United States to Costa Rica. Our major adjustment in San Jose was the learning of a new language. Since we studied and lived with other North Americans, our adjustment to the Latin culture did not precipitate a major cultural adaptation.

However, when we arrived in Colombia for a three-year term of service, our second bout with culture shock was much more complex and crippling. The list of differences between our birth culture and the Latin culture was extensive. We were taller and had a fairer complexion. Our poor Spanish crippled our communication and identified us as foreigners. The practices, mores, and customs of the Colombian culture sometimes aggravated me. For example, I was obsessive-compulsive about events starting on time while the Colombian view of time was much more relaxed. Events often began 30 minutes late.

We knew the cure for culture shock would not be found by changing the culture. The cure would come only with time and in a way or ways that no one could specify. One of the keys to our family's adaptation came in an unexpected way that no one could have scripted because of its authenticity and specificity.

Much of our shock revolved around the absence of genuine friendship. We often found that as husband and wife, we could not help one another with our unhappiness. Nearly all Colombians were friendly and considerate. But being friendly and being friends are two different things. Friendships can't be ordered through a mail-order catalogue. The best of friendships develop and are not planned. They can't be forced. Instead, they result when two or more people meet and wish to pursue spending more time together. Usually there is a common need or interest that finds a possible solution in the other person or persons.

Our emptiness in our new home far exceeded what we had anticipated. The "things" we brought from the United States didn't resolve loneliness. If I had known the pain and fears of adapting to a new culture and finding new friends, I would have wrestled with God about a call to leave my home for a new climate, home, foods, healthcare, laws, social practices, language, and holidays.

The Colombian church assigned me as pastor of a congregation of 200 in Armenia, Colombia. We worked with people every day. How can you be surrounded by so many people and yet feel so isolated? It didn't make sense. And then, "the sharing of a simple meal" became the first sight of light at the end of our lonely tunnel. It all began with a shoe salesman and his wife coming to visit our church. The greatest thing we had in common was our age. They lived in one room behind a shoe store. We lived in a three bedroom, three-bath upper-middle class community. However, from simple greetings and a few smiles, a mysterious wish for friendship developed.

William and Lucy Giraldo invited us to their apartment for lunch. We arrived and found that they had a bed, a small television, a table with two chairs, a hot plate, and two cabinets where they kept their clothes and personal items. There was a small bathroom at the far back of the room where they bathed and washed their dishes. No doubt they struggled daily to put food on their table. Their whole apartment was only slightly larger than our living room.

Our hosts insisted that we sit at their table on their chairs and they sat on chairs brought in from the shoe store as we ate. "We hope you like beans and rice!" Their initiative formally began a friendship that has lasted until this day. Thirty years after we left Colombia as missionaries, hardly a month goes by that I do not speak to them or one of their children. They live a thousand miles away but are some of the closest friends I have. This incredible family opened our world to a profound depth of love that transcended culture, nationality, education, and financial position. A special meal, given with love, was a defining moment that opened the door for our escape from loneliness and the bonds of culture shock.

Colombia 1976

"A Taxi Driver Becomes the Good Samaritan"

Strange things happen at strange places at strange times. You never know when a naked woman is going to burst into your hotel lobby. If people put themselves in novel circumstances, they should expect the unexpected. My wife and I were staying in the small town of Buga, Colombia, in 1976. This city of 100,000 people in the center of Cauca Valley boasts of two visits by Simon Bolivar and some huge sugar plantations. Its two major landmarks are The Basilica del Señor de los Milagros and the Guadalajara Hotel.

Buga is nearly halfway between Armenia and Cali. Since we lived in Armenia and often had meetings in Cali, we would stop for a night at the luxurious hotel for its charm, food, and swimming pool. Unfortunately, Buga is very hot in the summer and air-conditioning was not a part of luxury in the 1970s.

One evening at 10:30 I could not get our son David, then three, interested in going to sleep as we waited for the mountain breeze to slowly cool the valley. So, I carried him to the marble-walled lobby where a breeze had already lowered temperatures by at least ten degrees. I was not yet tired from rocking my son when I heard a woman scream, "My Lord, what am I going to do? Someone stole everything I have!" When she finally came into sight, I got a first hand view of her dilemma. She was naked except for tennis shoes and a blue t-shirt much too big for her. Her hair was wet and uncombed. She continued to the registration desk to request a room key. After a few more minutes of incoherent panic, she disappeared with the bellman. I assumed that someone had gotten into her room while she was in the shower and stolen most or all of her belongings.

The next morning I quietly slid out of bed for some alone time in the hotel lobby. After a cup of coffee and three rings of *pan de bono* (a cheese bread usually served hot out of the oven), a reluctant desk clerk inquired if I spoke both Spanish and English. He ushered me to the manager's office and I got a different look at the woman I had seen the night before. Very quickly she explained the events of the previous evening. Still in a panic, she and the manager wanted me to go to the local police station to file a report and recover a few of her items that had mysteriously appeared.

As we took a taxi along the crowded city streets, she shared the horror of her experiences the previous evening. The whole story began in Tampa, Florida. Vanessa was a successful real estate agent who had read about the increasing numbers of tourists exploring the plantations, jungles and magnetic cities of Colombia. As a single she had traveled widely around the U.S.A. and felt it was time to expand her horizon toward the South. Why not Colombia? She had met a lot of Colombians in Florida and most of them spoke some English, so surely she could make her way around Colombia without too many difficulties. She mapped out a few cities of interest and began to plan her first international vacation, including the rather exclusive Guadalajara Hotel in Buga.

It soon became obvious that she was naive and lacked a hint of common sense. Her evening began with a late dinner in the hotel where three dark-haired, handsome Colombian men talked to her from the next table. They turned on the charm. She succumbed and moved over to their table and visited over coffee and flan. Their English was highly accented, but better than her few words of Spanish. The men offered to take her around Buga during the evening and promised that they would invite her to one of their farms the following day for a first-hand look at a South American hacienda. They seemed so amiable that she saw a chance to spend one less day and evening struggling with the language. Who knows what she really had in mind? One thing for certain, she wasn't thinking about "personal" one-to-one evangelism.

Their first stop was a small bar along the Buga River. She remembered it was a thatch-covered building with a lot of bamboo beams left exposed inside. The place was vibrating with a loud band. The crowded tables had a mix of men and women, but there were many more men. Her new friends introduced Vanessa to the famous *aguardiente* of the country. This anise-flavored drink comes under many labels, but they all have a very high alcohol content. One bottle and shot glasses are distributed to each table and the result is not pretty. People often get boisterous and lose control over what they say and do. Poor Vanessa didn't remember a lot about the evening after the first hour.

She remembered the group suggesting the men walk her back to the hotel. The bar was only a short walk away. This walk along the avenue paralleled the river that also passed the Guadalajara Hotel. So, the group headed in the right direction. But Vanessa said she saw the river and wanted to "skinny-dip." The group watched as she stripped. Then, she remembered slipping on a slimy rock, and when she finally got up, no one responded to her call for help. So, she eventually made her way to the riverbank to recover her clothes; they were gone. Nothing remained of her purse, more than $500 in cash, traveler's checks, watch, airplane tickets, camera, or passport. Inebriated, she struggled up the riverbank to the sidewalk, totally bare except for her shoes. She didn't realize her plight. It was at this point, after being intoxicated by three fine men and left alone in a river to drown, that a taxi driver stopped to check out the spectacle and gave the woman his t-shirt to restore some modesty. He spoke no English, but she must have mentioned the Guadalajara Hotel. It was in that condition that I first saw the distraught woman.

The police were somewhat helpful. During the early morning the police had questioned a young, capricious romantic because of the complaint issued by the hotel, where the man frequently befriended single women. He claimed he knew nothing about what had happened to the woman after she decided to walk herself back to the hotel. However, during the night the police had recovered her traveler's checks, her hotel key, her passport, and her airplane tickets in a local park where someone had thrown them. The story was that one of the three men at the bar with Vanessa was actually a seminary student. When he left the bar, he walked home and by pure accident saw Vanessa's purse in a local park where someone must have left it. The police suggested that due to Vanessa's travel schedule and the recovery of the stolen items, it would be better she be on her way.

We met the man who gave the woman his shirt. It was clear that it was a wild experience for him to see a disoriented naked women standing along the street. Being a preacher, my mind went to the story of the Good Samaritan and felt the taxi driver's generosity worthy of remembering. And, I wondered, did God's "hand" influence the driver to have compassion on this wandering stranger?

Colombia 1976

"Another Missionary Christmas Story"

Most of the time my favorite color is not green. Christmas amends the rule. Christmas brings green and red from the color charts and predominantly marks them in my mind. I want to see and smell spruce. Christmas isn't quite right without those two indicators that the celebration of the birth of Jesus is near.

Life in el Quindio, the center of coffee plantations in Colombia, South America, brings green into view everywhere. You see the deep shining green of the coffee tree leaves and the more muted greens of the leaves of the platano and banana trees everywhere you drive. But, the spotting of a classical North American spruce or pine is nearly impossible; it is illegal to harvest them in Colombia. So, the evergreen Christmas tree is not a part of the decorations in Colombian homes during December.

The Watkins family always made a big deal about the search for the perfect tree. Dad would grab his double-edged ax, and my sis and I would follow his big footsteps in the snow. We always walked deep into the timber to find the right tree. The perfect trees never grew close to our house, but were hidden in deepest parts of the timber. We selected a tree based on color, a heavy fullness of its boughs, and a height that reached perfectly to the ceiling of our living room.

In Colombia, elaborate *pesebres* (nativity scenes) are front and center in most living rooms and churches. If you see a "Christmas tree," it is a simple limb severed from a hardwood tree and stuck into a five-gallon bucket. Each square inch of every branch is then covered with cotton. The result is a white tree decorated with lights and other colorful adornments. For me, the "swab" tree irritated more than helped in creating the spirit of Christmas. So, during our first treeless Christmas, my letters included brief complaints about the lack of a "proper" tree. In other words, in regard to Christmas trees, I failed to adjust to my new culture. I kept my discontent quiet around Colombians, but vented my feelings through writing.

As a rule, most North American churches have their share of sympathetic members. They take the needs of missionaries seriously. They have a spiritual dimension in their lives that allows them to see needs and compels them to respond with a solution. These people could be called "can-do" people. They make things happen. Betty Frazier was one of those people. She wrote us a letter nearly every week, reporting on her family and the "goings on" at the church I had pastored before leaving for Colombia. Simultaneously, we were sending our journals to Betty so she could understand our life on the mission field. No doubt our letters often rested in the same post office going in different directions.

Betty was distraught by our lack of a tree. She bought a $150 tree on half-price in January and spent a morning packaging it for the three-month journey by boat to Colombia via surface mail. Betty was very spontaneous, capable of both bouts of empathy and anger. Her postal clerk notified her that the post office couldn't mail her immense package to Colombia in one box. Instead, the post office required two smaller boxes. This information sent Betty into an instantaneous rant about the government's unnecessary regulations and exploitation of the public, leaving the clerk in a nervous sweat in the middle of winter.

Later the same day Betty returned to the same post office, tugging her two boxes behind her. She was not smiling when she pushed them over the counter and into the emotionally bruised chest of the reluctant clerk. This time the packages met the code for size and weight. But the news that the cost for surface mail would be $78.75 stunned Betty. That was more than she had paid for the discounted tree. Again, she delivered a blistering review of the United States Postal Service and made it clear that she wanted her complaint passed to the proper authorities including Tennessee's Republican senators, Brock and Baker.

The Christmas tree arrived in early July. There were two massive cardboard boxes, apparently gift-wrapped with more than 100 postage stamps of small denominations, all carefully placed by Betty's loving hands. We gladly paid the $30 custom fee and returned to our home knowing our 1977 tree would be green, the "authentic" color for a Christmas tree.

Colombia 1977

"Mi Familia Me Botó"

Memories can be painful, even when they surface after decades. My notes from November 1977 reminded me of a visit I made to the one-room musty smelling apartment of a man I will call—Don Pedro. It took him two or three minutes to shuffle across the termite-infested floor to the rain-stained door. I was stopping to invite him to a men's workshop in the neighbor city of Pereira.

The walls were unpainted. Much of the adobe plaster had fallen away, exposing the bamboo sub-structure. One picture—"*El Sagado Corazón de Jesus*"—depicted Jesus with his heart clearly visible, superimposed on his body, and surrounded by a halo effect, driving the observer's eyes first to heart, then to the face of Jesus. This type of Christian art still shocked me despite my two years in Latin America. The picture tilted to the left perhaps from the last tremor so common in the mountain towns of Colombia.

I said, "Are you planning on attending the conference this weekend in Pereira?" He responded, "I can't. I have no one to take me; "*Mi familia me botó hace años*." (My family threw me away years ago.) I learned in the following moments that Don Pedro's divorce thirty years previous had resulted not only with the loss of his wife, but his entire family had abandoned him following bouts of anger, blame, hate, and resentment. His hands trembled as he spoke of the pain and brokenness.

As he spoke honestly about his horrible mistakes, I silently begged God for a miracle that could lead to forgiveness and reconciliation. I struggled to invent a way to resolve this man's sadness. How could anyone endure the pain of a complete separation from one's children and extended family? What would it take for his children to forgive him before he died? Would he once again see the smile of his son and daughter? Would God work a miracle and help heal these broken relationships? Would some person step up and help this family to do the right thing?

Colombia 1977

"Hot Air Balloons on a Bus"

Some people have asked me when and where and why I have been most frightened in my work in third world countries. I am sort of fatalistic; I try not to fear that which might come. So it is not a part of me to worry in anticipation of trips. Instead, my fear rises when I gradually lose control about whether I can wisely avoid or escape danger. I remember a few incidents of fear, but really not many considering the amount of travel I have had into countries (like Liberia, Myanmar, Colombia, China, Laos) often declared as dangerous by the U.S. Department of State.

I did have one moment of controllable fear during a bus ride outside of Aguadas, Antioquia, Colombia. You have to know a person's background and the particular context at a given time of fear to understand it fully. What precipitates fear in one person won't even be an issue for another. The 1970s in Colombia were the very tail end of three decades of emotional and physical persecution of the evangelical church by the Conservative Party and the Roman Catholic Church. The 1930s, 40s and 50s had been horrible for Protestant converts and evangelical missionaries. History records the burning of churches as well as the stoning, castration, and martyrdom of Protestant believers.

(Note: I am writing these reflections from the normative Protestant prospective of the 1970s. This problem was a result of what Roman Catholics viewed as the Protestant churches' proselytism of their members. Their view rested on the assumption that anyone born into a Roman Catholic family by default became Roman Catholic.

Therefore, Protestant pastors, laity, or missionaries should not approach their followers with a different perspective on the Christian faith. Protestants, on the other hand, often viewed Roman Catholics as not having a personal relationship with Jesus Christ, but rather as people that saw faith as only important at key events in life such as birth, baptism, marriage, and death.)

The antagonism between Roman Catholics and Protestants ranged from minimal to intense, depending on the location and the ecumenical spirit of leaders. Unfortunately, many threats aimed only to raise fear occasionally flamed into a tragic or deadly event. Thankfully, by the time we moved to Colombia in 1975, the vicious attacks against evangelicals had slackened to a lot more bark than bite.

Large cities like Bogotá and Cali were basically locations of religious peace. The Protestant and the Roman Catholic Church had progressed to ignoring each other rather than constantly degrading and denying the spiritual validity of the other.

However, in some rural pockets where there were no Protestant churches, a very small number of priests still encouraged their members to threaten evangelists with the strategy that fear would drive Protestants from the smaller rural villages.

The days of isolation declined as more and more families heard and believed the importance of a personal relationship with Christ. These new converts were full of passion and audacity. Their public testimonies of faith led to having their businesses boycotted. New believers were often denied equal access to jobs. Most towns and villages had two cemeteries, one for Roman Catholics and another for Protestants because most priests would not allow evangelicals to be buried in church-run cemeteries.

Such hostility was totally unknown to me. I grew up in Iowa as a part of the majority—a white, Anglo-Saxon, Protestant. In retrospect, I seldom considered my historic roots, my specific faith, or my race. Most Iowans were either Anglo-Saxons or Native Americans. People talked the same, looked the same, and acted the same. It was rare for Roman Catholics to marry Protestants, but certainly not forbidden. The few minorities were so limited in numbers that they hardly caused a second thought, let alone a threat to anyone that I knew. My world was pretty much painted some tone of white. No doubt, prejudices loomed under some surfaces but the opportunity for discrimination seldom arose.

My life as a North American missionary, living in Colombia, placed me in the minority more times than not. It was more an inconvenience than a problem with painful repercussions. I was tall; the indigenous population was short. That was no problem except for mowing off a few light bulbs in houses with lower ceilings. I was a Protestant, 97% of the people identified themselves as Roman Catholics. Our family was fortunate to live in an upper middle class neighborhood where religious preference was not important. I preferred American football, most people adored soccer. I quickly adjusted and prefer soccer to this day. I was strangely fair-skinned in comparison to the darker mestizo coloring of many Colombians. I usually felt accepted, but there were a few exceptions.

The town of Aguadas is mid-way between Manizales and Medellin on the western *cordillera* of the Andes. There were four ways into the city of Aguadas: bus, car, horse, and on foot. The mountain roads were treacherous because of the narrow, curving gravel roads and deviant driving. It was not at all unusual to approach a sharp curve and look toward the other side of the chasm only to see a rusted out shell of a vehicle that had obviously crashed years ago after being forced off the road. I learned that one principle of driving determined the difference between life and death. People just assumed that if you needed to pass, it was okay to start the pass regardless of the distance of visibility. However, if a car appeared and if you were not side-by-side to the vehicle being passed, you must hit the brakes and return to a place behind the vehicle you were passing. On the other hand, if a driver moved ahead of side-by-side and another vehicle appeared, it was the approaching driver who braked and allowed the pass. Usually, the system worked. Despite the danger of driving a car under those conditions, it beat riding a bus in the rural areas. Buses were never retired in Colombia; their owners sold them to companies servicing more dangerous highways. Now, that was insane logic. Take an aging bus with an antiquated, leaking brake system, a defunct suspension, and tires with little to no tread, and put it on gravel mountain roads with 180 degree hairpin turns; it is a miracle that disasters did not occur with regular frequency.

So, I would drive my 1975 mustard-colored Land Rover into Aguadas, park it, and take one of the rickety old *escaleras* (buses) burdened with people, animals, and baggage to the end of the line where we would walk to the mountain farms where no vehicles could enter.

On one such trip I arrived in Aguadas late at night and spent the night with Anna and Pedro, some of the first Protestants of the village. Early mornings in Aguadas were frigid. The little village was known as the town of the mist. Even the locals hated to roll out of bed, but when they did they quickly shifted from a blanket to a *ruana* (a wool poncho). The coffee and *pandebono* (cheese bread) and *arepa* venders were the first to leave the limited warmth of the home.

I always hated to take a shower during those visits because it meant shivering in the 40-60 °F degree bathroom and then drying with a minuscule towel. The real hitch with a shower in homes with some financial resources for upgrades was the so-called shower heater. Many people called the little apparatus a "widow maker." Houses had no water heaters. Instead, they had a gizmo inserted in the water pipe between where it came out of the wall and above the showerhead. Somehow, this coil reached a very high temperature and slightly heated the water. To turn this invention on, you needed to be wearing rubber flip-flops to create a ground; then the user pulled a toggle switch on the wall inside the shower stall. When the toggle made proper contact and closed the circuit, sparks would fly in every direction. If you felt nothing, you thanked God for another warm shower; if not, you got a jolt through your body that either adjusted your spinal column or sent you quickly to meet your Maker. I hated the danger of flipping the switch, but not as much I detested a freezing shower.

After recovering from hypothermic bathroom syndrome, Anna always served a breakfast second to none.

I could have endured a swim in the Arctic Ocean to get to those breakfasts. Anna knew how to make a *perico* (a scrambled egg) like none other—just the right amount of onions, tomatoes and cilantro, folded into the eggs and cooked until just beyond unhealthy. Scoop that on a plate with a couple of slices of farmer's cheese, a crisp *arepa* smothered with butter, a homemade *chorizo*, and who could ask for anything more? During such meals I wondered why I received a salary.

As I finished my breakfast, Anna brought her *loro* (parrot) to the table for its breakfast. Come to find out, the medium-sized green *loro* had not learned to eat by itself. She had raised the bird from the time it hatched, and began serving the bird with a tiny coffee spoon, eventually graduating to a teaspoon. The bird was three years old but would not eat from a seed tray like most birds.

I used Aguadas as a launching point for ten days of visits to rural coffee farms scattered all over the mountains northeast of Aguadas.

From the town square we boarded an *escalera* for an hour ride to the end of the road at *Tres Esquinas* (Three Corners). Aguadas was known for its escaleras. These colorful buses were entirely rebuilt starting with nothing but a retired chassis. They were primarily wooden constructs with a floor and seats mounted on top of a bus chassis. The creative touch on each bus relied on the bright colors the builder chose for his prize. The owner usually painted a landscape on the back of the bus for other drivers to enjoy as they followed them up and down the mountains. Each bus had its own unique name such as "Manual's Chariot" or "Antonio's Welcome Wagon." My bus left at 8:30 a.m. daily, or when no more people could climb aboard. It was always comical to see a pig tied to the bus, just above the bumper.

Little did I know I was about to take the ride in the seat in front of two farmhands bent on spoiling my day. Approximately twenty passengers can find a wooden pew inside the bus, and a similar number will also often be found sitting on the luggage strapped to the flat top built for cargo. Another six to eight people cling on for dear life to the back while standing on the bumper and you have a sight—a tragedy waiting to happen.

You could never truly relax on these trips because of the hard seats and bumpy roads. This hour ride into the hinterland began harmlessly until I allowed myself to listen to the conversation going on behind me. "I wonder what these religious imperialists from the U.S.A. would look like hanging by their feet from an avocado tree?" "Why don't those damned Protestants realize they aren't wanted here?" "Maybe a few of these Gringo preachers need to disappear...that might end their visits where they aren't invited." I didn't want to turn around to check the size and age of the speakers. I was certain they meant their words for the tall North American directly in front of them. The tone of their voices led me to guess they were teenagers and a physical threat, but also uncertain about themselves. I knew they would have a sharp machete attached to their belts since this was standard for all coffee farmers. I prayed they intended to scare me and not follow through on their threats. However, I evaluated my options. Should I hang around the drop point where there was a small store? Should I leave immediately toward the first farm I would visit and hope I could run faster than they? I really didn't like either of my options that well. But upon arrival, they quickly jumped off the bus and walked away from me. So, I hung around the store long enough to drink a cup of coffee and then headed for Don David's house. And, that was the end of that—just two hot air balloons that disappeared into the coffee plants.

Colombia 1978

"The Day Jaime Decided to Become a Missionary"

Coping with drunks in worship services in a middle-class suburban church in North America infrequently becomes a problem, but in Colombian churches it often occurs. Churches are commonly on the same street or around the corner from bars, nightclubs, and houses of prostitution. Odds are high that sooner or later some drunk will stumble into the open door of the church for a look. Drunks are somewhat like cats; their curiosity drives them where they would not normally go. Sometimes, they will fall in love with the quiet, accepting atmosphere and decide to return with frequency.

I always felt tense when some "unknown" character swayed down the aisle. It was perplexing to await their problematic response to something holy and sacred. Sometimes, they tried to contradict my sermon or criticize some Protestant practice. Other times, they were a harmless, humorous distraction as they mimicked a church clown and then disappeared as quickly as they had come. The most pathetic cases were the winos who attended and tried to participate with their stunned senses and uninhibited behavior. My response from the beginning was to go on as best as practically possible, ignoring them and praying for their quick exit.

Evangelical Christians are respectful of the sanctity of the sanctuary—no running, no eating or drinking, and no outbursts of noise. They demand reverence from their children and others in the temple of God. The Armenia Church was a large Gothic structure that would seat close to two hundred people, including the balcony, so one drunk could wobble in without a lot of notice as long as he was quiet. But when an intoxicated person threatened the solemnity of a service, the church leadership responded promptly and with force.

Mr. Jaime was our most frequent visitor to the Armenia Church. He appeared at least once a month; most of the time he just took his place in the first pew and sat quietly as if he had no idea of where he was or why he was there. I am convinced that he usually didn't. He was often blitzed beyond sensibility. He was a shriveled raisin of a man who didn't weigh more than 130 pounds. He probably survived on the calories he imbibed. He was really a pathetic creature, obviously demented from his years of alcoholism. The smashed fellow, with his dilapidated shoebox, would stumble down a side aisle to the first pew and find a place among the young people of the church who congregated in that section to assist with the music. It was quite a site to see the old fellow integrate himself into the smallest gap among the considerate, amused, and defenseless youth.

All the people within six feet were aware of Jaime even if he entered during a prayer. There was the shuffling and flopping of his soles that had come loose from the rest of his shoes and the stifling body odor that saturated his clothes. His own odor was so penetrating that it masked the smell of the alcohol on his breath. His situation was so vile it caused nausea for many who were seated nearby.

Poor Jaime never fully understood what was going on; we were never able to get him sober enough to know the real person behind the smell. (Even today as I write I can still sense the horrible odor.) His shoebox only contained one item—a copy of the Jehovah Witness *Watchtower* magazine. It always unnerved me a bit as I began to preach to see him pull it out.

Two vivid incidents stand out in my mind in relation to Jaime: the day he attempted to replace the elders of the church and the morning he came to the altar with a personal decision.

In the Armenia church the custom for serving Holy Communion was for the pastor to hand the bread and wine to four elders who then served the rest of the believers. On one particular Sunday, I called for the elders to come forward to prepare the Lord's Table. I was startled to see four church leaders and Jaime come forward! I instructed the four to go ahead and serve; I asked Jaime to stand to one side. My hope was to avoid a spectacle. But, Jaime had other plans. He loudly insisted with his normal slur that he had come forward to serve. *"Yo vooy a serviirr laa santaa ceena."* (I am going to serve Holy Communion.)

That did it! Two of the leaders acted quickly to bodily remove him from the premises. Again, Jaime decided that he would not be moved without a fight—a skirmish quickly developed. His cursing was much clearer than his normal conversation. The more the elders fought to move him, the more he squirmed and twisted and flung his arms. We finally calmed him from combat mode and were able to persuade him to take a seat in a pew with the insinuation that he could help me more from the pew. But, obviously, the dignity and spirit of the celebration of the love and sacrifice of Jesus had been lost. People didn't know whether to laugh or cry. Everyone was perplexed and mystified over how we should minister to this poor child of God.

Several months later in March of 1978, we were making an effort to recruit two young single men to leave their homes and serve as workers among the Cholo Indians in the jungles along the San Juan River. I was preaching on the missionary call and could sense that God's spirit was moving during the service. Attention was intense and I discerned a spiritual conviction in the eyes of several.

As I concluded, I emphasized: "God needs two young men willing to leave their families to serve as his servants and evangelists among the Cholo Indians." Immediately, three of our finest youth came forward. As I spoke with them I saw another person start forward. I cried to myself, "Oh God, don't let this ruin this moment for your glory." I quietly approached Jaime and asked him, "Jaime, what is it that you want?" To which he whispered, "I am ready to go to the Cholos as a missionary." My mind went into high gear. How was I to moderate this potential disaster? Instead of trying to dissuade him, I said, "Very good, Jaime. God bless you." As I looked to the crowd and called them to prayer, I could see that slight grin on the mouths of those who had heard what had been said. I closed the service thankful that most people had no idea of the content of our conversation.

Jaime never made it to the San Juan River, but he did continue to return to one of his favorite pews. But, since then, I have wondered—*Should I have handled Jaime's attending our church differently? How spiritually sensitive are people we perceive to be just too different from ourselves? Was our forgiving and loving God trying to speak to Jaime? Was his obedience a remnant of a past faith?*

No Particular Place—Any Specific Time

"The Society for the Picking of Apples"

Are you familiar with the parable Jesus told about the lost sheep? Here is a different perspective on the same need.

"Once upon a time there was an apple grower who had acres and acres of apple trees. In all, he had 10,000 acres of apple orchards. One day he went to the nearby town. There, he hired 1,000 apple pickers. He told them:

'Go to my orchards. Harvest the ripe apples, and build storage buildings for them so that they will not spoil. I need to be gone for a while, but I will provide all you will need to complete the task. When I return, I will reward you for your work. I'll set up a Society for the Picking of Apples. This Society to which you will all belong will be responsible for the entire operation. Naturally, in addition to those of you doing the actual harvesting, some will carry supplies, others will care for the physical needs of the group, and still others will have administrative responsibilities.'

As he set up the Society structure, some people volunteered to be pickers and others to be packers. Others put their skills to work as truck drivers, cooks, accountants, storehouse builders, apple inspectors, and even administrators. Every one of his workers could, of course, have picked apples. In the end, however, only 100 of the 1,000 employees wound up as full-time pickers. The 100 pickers started harvesting immediately. Ninety-four of them began picking around the homestead. The remaining six looked out toward the horizon. They decided to head out to the far-away orchards.

Before long, the 94 pickers with beautiful, delicious apples had filled the storehouses on the 800 acres immediately surrounding the homestead.

The orchards on the 800 acres around the homestead had thousands of apple trees. But with almost all of the pickers concentrating on them, those trees were soon picked nearly bare. In fact, the ninety-four apple pickers working around the homestead began having difficulty finding trees that had not been picked.

As the apple picking slowed around the homestead, Society members began channeling their efforts into building larger storehouses and developing better equipment for picking and packing. They even started some schools to train prospective apple pickers to replace those who one day would be too old to pick apples.

Sadly, those ninety-four pickers working around the homestead began fighting among themselves. Incredible as it may sound, some began stealing apples that had already been picked. Although there were enough trees on the 10,000 acres to keep every available worker busy, those working nearest the homestead failed to move into unharvested areas. They just kept working those 800 acres nearest the house. Some on the northern edge sent their trucks to get apples on the southern side. And those on the south side sent their trucks to gather on the east side.

Even with all that activity, the harvest on the remaining 9,200 acres was left to just six pickers. Those six were, of course, far too few to gather all the ripe fruit in those thousands of acres. So, by the hundreds of thousands, apples rotted on the trees and fell to the ground.

One of the students at the apple-picking school showed a special talent for picking apples quickly and effectively. When he heard about the thousands of acres of untouched faraway orchards, he started talking about going there.

His friends discouraged him. They said: 'Your talents and abilities make you very valuable around the homestead. You'd be wasting your talents out there. Your gifts can help us harvest apples from the trees on our central 800 acres more rapidly. That will give us more time to build bigger and better storehouses. Perhaps you could even help us devise better ways to use our big storehouses since we have wound up with more space than we need for the present crop of apples.'

With so many workers and so few trees, the pickers and packers and truck drivers—and all the rest of the Society for the Picking of Apples living around the homestead—had time for more than just picking apples.

They built nice houses and raised their standard of living. Some became very conscious of clothing styles. Thus, when the six pickers from the far-off orchards returned to the homestead for a visit, it was apparent that they were not keeping up with the styles in vogue with the other apple pickers and packers.

To be sure, those on the homestead were always good to those six who worked in the far away orchards. When any of those six returned from the far away fields, they were given the red carpet treatment. Nonetheless, those six pickers were saddened that the Society of the Picking of Apples spent 96 percent of its budget for bigger and better apple-picking methods and equipment and personnel for the 800 acres around the homestead while it spent only 4 percent of its budget on all those distant orchards.

To be sure, those six pickers knew that an apple is an apple wherever it may be picked. They knew that the apples around the homestead were just as important as apples far away. Still, they could not erase from their minds the sight of thousands of trees, which had never been touched by a picker.

They longed for more pickers to come help them. They longed for help from packers, truck drivers, supervisors, equipment-maintenance men, and ladder builders. They wondered if the professionals working back around the homestead could teach them better apple-picking methods so that, out where they worked, fewer apples would rot and fall to the ground.

Those six sometimes wondered to themselves whether or not the Society for the Picking of Apples was doing what the orchard owner had asked it to do.

While one might question whether the Society was doing what the owner wanted done, the members did keep very busy. Several members were convinced that proper apple picking requires nothing less than the very best equipment. Thus, the Society assigned several members to develop bigger and better ladders as well as nicer boxes to store apples. The Society also prided itself at having raised the qualification level for full-time apple pickers.

When the owner returns, the Society members will crowd around him. They'll proudly show off the bigger and better ladders they've built and the nice apple boxes they've designed and made. One wonders how happy that owner will be, however, when he looks out and sees the acres and acres of untouched trees with their unpicked apples."[2]

Colombia 1978

"Not Going to the Dogs"

Many people debate whether God actually exists. Others question God's involvement in the world. One question creates another. Could God possibly give a hoot about what happens to each and every human being? How could God possibly be pursuing a friendship with each person? Our daily walks through life allow us to see the presence of something much bigger than ourselves. Experience confirms soundly that God does actively enter into the lives of the people made in his image. My personal experiences of travel have confirmed that.

I used to explore the Andes Mountains in search of people who were already Christians to encourage their relationship with Christ. Or, I would attempt to meet individuals who had not yet understood the impact that the gospel could have on their life. This particular strategy was sort of pushed on me by the nature of my work as a missionary. All full-time ministers were expected to take ten-day trips annually into this area around Aguadas, Colombia, to evangelize and disciple.

No one I knew went there for pleasure. These mountains were so steep that it required incredible energy and stamina to hike from one small poor farm to another. Those were the days when the farmers had never heard of refrigerators or ice, so even in the heat of the sun, we had to settle for a glass of warm water. These were the poor coffee farmers of Colombia. They eked out a living raising coffee, platanos, yucca, and small livestock on a few acres of land. Almost all families lived in damp, dirt-floored two or three room houses made with a type of adobe. Since these families had inhabited this land for generations, the houses were generally in a sad state of repair with only the roof receiving the necessary care to keep the family dry.

The kitchens were fascinating. They consisted only of a creative oven that somehow contained a wood fire that burned sixteen to twenty hours a day. This brick vault was covered with half-inch metal sheets on which all types of pots and pans sat. The remainder of the top of the vault was open and allowed the flames to rise at times above the grated surface. It was here that arepas (a type of bread) could be prepared or meat could be grilled. Food was constantly being prepared for one of the five meals offered each day.

I was stunned the first time I wandered into this center of strange but inviting smells. Men seldom entered the kitchens; in fact, I don't recall seeing a coffee farmer in one of these rural food factories. Instead, only women of the family rushed in and out with food to be prepared or the results to be served. Humorously, when the women exited the kitchen, the bravest of the chickens would sneak into the kitchen to hop onto the edge of the stove and sneak a sample of whatever happened to be nearly prepared. I noticed one red-feathered hen, one of their cherished layers, sticking her beak into the boiling *sancocho*. This soup was made from chicken or beef, platanos, yucca, potatoes, celery, and a number of spices unique to each cook. Ironically, the meat was chicken. These brave birds were literally eating a part of their own without realizing that someday, they were destined to fall, piece by piece, into that same pot. If the chicken could have thought, it would have hightailed it any time a visitor arrived at the farm. Seldom do I remember a farm visit without chicken being served in one form or another.

But all of this was a rabbit chase to arrive at the story I set out to tell. We knew a majority of the farmers in the areas we frequented in the area east of the town of Aguadas. Each farmhouse had stories that one or another of the itinerant ministers had added to the folklore of the area's ministry. Many of the tales were undoubtedly embellished, but no one cared; they made good table talk. Some of the women were known as good cooks and others were skirted at mealtime, if at all possible. For me, the cleanliness issue was more important than the palate. A stop at Anna Maria's house was simply nothing to brag about. Her hands were always caked with several levels of dirt from garden work. It took my utmost effort to watch her pat out the bread into small pancake-shaped patties that would then be toasted over the open flames, then smothered in butter and salted liberally. None of these women had ever seen a recipe book. Instead, they learned from a chain of mothers, spanning over centuries. I suspect little had changed over the years—the biggest culinary discovery that had been added was probably when salt was first discovered under the Andes Mountains.

One spring morning we had risen early and caught the best meal of the day at Reynaldo's house. There was little better than a crisp *arepa* and fresh eggs scrambled to perfection. I don't understand why, but scrambled eggs are always better at a home where many children are present. The more eggs broken in the skillet, the better the flavor. I have been told an egg is a delicate product and the slower they cook, the tastier. Reinaldo's wife knew the perfect moment to pull them from the cast-iron skillet and place them on the plate with the small piece of meat that had been salted and hung in the kitchen, and then grilled precisely to go with the eggs. The eggs were still partly runny, a rich steaming pile of yellow.

Most of the time we hiked from farm to farm, using the small paths that had been worn by humans, horses, and beasts of burden. Each farm had these small paths that linked it to other farms and eventually to the closest village, often hours away. As we avoided twisting an ankle in one of the ruts, I noticed a small farmhouse perhaps five minutes down the path. We had passed this farm on former trips, but I had avoided trying to make contact with the residents. This farm had a reputation for its uncontrollable dogs. The place was a rustic, gated community. The owners had built a six-foot fence around the entire yard surrounding the modest adobe house.

Since the house was built on the side of the mountain, we had a fair idea of the layout from our decline down the mountain. The mountain was so steep that we had actually looked right into the yard as we descended. Nothing had moved except the kitchen smoke.

That day I suggested to Gustavo that we should try to make contact with the family and invite them to attend our preaching service at Jose's house that night. Most of these families would walk miles to have some social contact. We approached the front gate and peered through the fence constructed of bamboo poles about the size of a person's finger and stripped of twigs. These poles were attached to larger bamboo trunks planted in the ground as the supporting infrastructure. We banged on the gate to get someone's attention, but nothing stirred. The only living creature in sight was a bulky dog snoozing near the kitchen door. He seemed to care little that we were there. The yard was pretty much barren of habitation, a dirt lot that must have become a mud flat during the rainy season.

This particular day I was daring and decided to open the gate and walk into the yard to try to stir someone. After crossing the midway point toward the actual door on which I planned to knock on, the sleeping German shepherd suddenly became aware of an intruder. He rose in a flash and charged right toward me, showing too many teeth and barking sharply. I froze instantly, more from fear than a conscious decision. Then the unbelievable happened. The enraged dog passed me as if it had never seen me and charged the gateway where my friend awaited. Gustavo slammed the gate in time to separate himself from the animal that could have easily removed an arm with one bite and twist. I might as well have been a lamb in front of a starved lion. I remained frozen with no way to escape. I stood in place with my head turned to anticipate the next charge of the dog. There was no doubt in my mind that I would soon be the target. I actually remember praying, "Please let someone come and save me." But no one appeared. The dog finally quit jumping against the gate and even settled into silence. When he felt the gatekeeper was no threat to his territory, he turned and returned to his original place on the ground near the abandoned kitchen. He walked within inches of me but neither smelled nor saw me. I waited until he sprawled out and then I bolted quickly to the gate and escaped without a scratch. But I was stunned by the occasion and will always believe that God struck the dog blind to preserve my welfare. Some would say it was a coincidence, that the dog had overlooked me in his focus to attack my friend. I doubt that. It is hard to miss a six-foot "scarecrow."

These experiences cause one to wonder about the "protective umbrellas" that cover us in such dangerous situations. They can't be explained. But I choose to thank God for daily protection and guidance. And, I learn more and more that we have to be cautious about the circumstances in which we place ourselves.

Today, terrorism provides another scenario for travelers. However, though I have chosen to be careful about travel, I still have to depend on the umbrella of God's care to have a sense of tranquility moving from one nation to another in these perilous days.

U.S.A. 1979

"Emmaus Road Experience"

Years ago I had an "Emmaus Road Experience." Jesus had an incident following his resurrection when two of his disciples were walking along the Emmaus road and were joined by the risen Jesus. They didn't recognize him until they sat down to have dinner together.

In my case, I had come back from the mission field and gone by the furniture company where my mom worked. After a good visit, she suggested, "Why don't you go down and wait for your dad when he comes out of the factory?" So, I did.

I heard the company whistle announcing the shift change. I leaned up against a concrete post at the gate to watch for dad. In a little bit I sighted him, flowing forward in the tide of men rushing for their pickups and cars. He passed right by me, within a yard; I could have reached out and touched him. His kind eyes were fixed straight ahead and he never saw me. I fell in behind and soon caught up to his side. He was really hoofing it to his pickup. I said, "Hey man, you're in a hurry today." He replied, "Yep, my son's coming home from South America and I got to get home!" We chatted for a few more seconds but he never looked toward me. I was tickled with his intensity, sort of numb to anything outside his point of concentration. It was not until I put my arm around his shoulders that he glanced over and recognized me as his son.

Sometimes, God puts the important in a place that is so unexpected that we overlook it. Perhaps, we need to slow down and look carefully for the voice and direction of God.

U.S.A. 1980

"The Child's Mite"

"As Jesus looked up, he saw the rich putting their gifts into the temple treasury. He also saw a poor widow put in two very small copper coins. 'Truly I tell you,' he said, 'this poor widow has put in more than all the others. All these people gave their gifts out of their wealth; but she out of her poverty put in all she had to live on'" (Luke 21:1-4).

We have many of the same sentiments and feelings as God. The fact that we are created in the image of God gives us that assurance.

On an unusually cold day in January in Tampa, Florida, I made a missionary visit to the Macedonia congregation, a Hispanic New Church Development Project. Exactly seventeen people came to hear my presentation about the work on the Colombian mission field. A memory stands out vividly from the visit.

I highlighted the fact that 300 children die daily in Colombia of malnutrition and urged those present to make a personal contribution to our denominational hot lunch program to help alleviate some of hunger faced by people due to no fault of their own. After the program, a little boy waited in line to talk to me. He handed me 44 pennies. I hope I never forget the joy on his face as he said, "Please use this for one of the children." Why he had the money with him, I will never know. But, since he was the son of a migrant worker, I'm relatively certain that he contributed every cent he had to his name. I better understood Jesus' overwhelming joy when he saw a widow make a gift to the temple treasury of the only two coins to her name. Giving one's all is the greatest of sacrifice.

U.S.A. 1980

"The Conversion of a Dump"

A group of believers in Tennessee built a beautiful church on a small hill on a bypass around Clarksville. I remember the area before the church was erected. It was an eyesore—a community dump, full of empty cans, bottles, stinking rags, old tires, discarded lumber, etc. At some point, the city government closed the pit and covered the ugly offal with fill dirt and then sodded the area. Eventually, a church was constructed on top of this rather dubious past and shifting foundation.

Unfortunately, the dump never fully disappeared. It would periodically raise its ugly face. The old nature popped out, so to speak. The last time I passed the church, I noticed an old tire had appeared at the base of the hill where rain had washed away the fill. As I drove away, I wondered when someone would stop on the way to church and remove the old tire. It didn't belong there, or did it? Was it a reminder of the past, beneficial for the present? Isn't this really a reminder of the ongoing nature of mission—sanctification is really a process rather than a moment of time.

I also wondered what old "whiskey bottle" would pop up next in my life? When it does surface, I am thankful the price has already been paid to haul the garbage from my dump.

China 1980

"Where Should We Evangelize?"

Chinese Christians have witnessed dramatic shifts in their freedom to worship in the last century. I visited China several times since my first exposure in 1980 when we were only allowed to look across the border from Hong Kong's New Territories into the mainland. That was four years after Mao's death; and since that historic event, China has gradually experimented with different strategies to permit, yet control, religious freedom. However, tracing religious freedom further back in history finds Christians severely persecuted during the wars and shifts in political ideologies. During the Cultural Revolution, 1966 to 1976, Mao effectively banned religious expression, and drove all religions underground. In 1979 the government restored the Three-Self Patriotic Movement, a government sanctioned framework for the public expression of the Protestant faith.

I have been privileged to preach in Three-Self churches on various occasions and have felt free to proclaim the truth of scriptures with two exceptions—it was assumed that the pulpit would not be used as a platform to criticize the Chinese government. Despite this unspoken restraint, I was always humored by jokes told by our government guides about their own government and its restraints upon the church. I could never fully decipher whether this was a subtle seduction for us to make similar comments, thereby putting our visit in jeopardy, or was simply the status quo for people with small amounts of power to joke carefully about their government.

Another written and spoken restriction was defined for us—we were not to attempt to evangelize or promote our faith outside the physical church structures. In other words, we could not get involved in any so-called "street evangelism." I found that sad. However, it was ironic that I lived in a country where people were free to share my testimony anywhere at anytime, yet most sharing of the Gospel occurred in the church and around other Christians, just as in China.

U.S.A. 1980

"Could Prayer Be the Only Answer?"

Not many people would choose, of their own volition, to be alienated from their parents. It happened to me. The year was 1980 and I was riding on a high because I had returned from my first four years on the mission field in Colombia, South America. There was a mystic about being a missionary, and I was anxious to share my experiences through visits to local churches. The year involved an incredible amount of travel. I visited nearly 150 local churches from California to Florida. In my zeal to be "The Missionary," I unintentionally disregarded some higher responsibilities.

The whole situation came crashing down when I had been in the states for ten months and attended the General Assembly of our denomination in Tulsa, Oklahoma. I was excited because my parents also were scheduled to attend the meeting. But, when I met my mother walking toward me in the hotel corridor, she walked right past me without as much as a smile. I reeled in the hall and followed her step-by-step to her room.

She allowed me into the room, but was absolutely quiet. I questioned her, "What's wrong Mom?" She still ignored me. "Come on, Mom, what's bugging you?" She quietly responded, "Oh, you want to know what is wrong? I will tell you. You have been in the states for nearly a year, traveling all over the country. But you have only found time for your dad and me on two occasions. I am angry with you, and I have no intention of forgiving you!"

My mind weighed her words and their consequences. I would be returning to Colombia in less than a month. If this chasm between the two of us couldn't be reconciled, I wasn't certain I could even return to service. I pleaded. "Mom, I have been so thoughtless. Please forgive me." Her response burned like steaming water being poured over my heart. She looked straight in the eyes and said, "You don't deserve to be forgiven."

We talked for another hour or so, but no progress was made toward restoring the love and understanding we had always felt. Finally, I gave up and said, "Mom, I think we need to get a pastor to help us." She was half-heartedly agreeable. Our church's minister was also present, so I began the search to find him. He was in his room and agreed to try to mediate the divide between the two of us. His effort was a total failure. Eventually, he confessed that he could not help us. Mom had set her emotions in concrete and was not about to shift her position. By then I was near panic.

I was exhausted. I felt totally hopeless. "Mom!" I said. "I am at my wit's end. I suggest we just get down on our knees and pray. Let's both just pray." I don't remember who prayed first, but we each prayed for the situation. When we were finished, we stood up. Mom looked at me and said, "I don't know what happened, but I feel totally relieved. I can forgive you…everything is going to be okay." God had done for us what we could not do for ourselves.

"All this is from God, who reconciled us to himself through Christ and gave us the ministry of reconciliation: that God was reconciling the world to himself in Christ, not counting men's sins against them…We are therefore Christ's ambassadors, as though God were making his appeal through us. We implore you on Christ's behalf: Be reconciled to God" (2 Corinthians 5:18-20).

Colombia 1982

"Should I or Shouldn't I?"

The call from the U.S.A. was crackling from a bad international phone connection, which was so common in the 1980s. With repetition I finally got the import of the conversation. Mr. Nicks, a retiree from

Tennessee, inquired about the advisability of spending $1,500 for travel expenses to do carpenter work at a food distribution site for children in Cali, Colombia, South America. My response popped out of my mouth, "Yes, by all means, come; you will never regret the decision."

Considerable discussion exists about the value of mission work trips. People ask, "Should I spend the money for plane tickets and other expenses to do volunteer service in a country other than my own, or should I write a check for a given project and allow those on the field to hire a national worker to do the same work I would do as a volunteer? It is a complex question, the answer to which is not as obvious as one might think! Actually, as with so many things, both options are correct.

For the sake of discussion, let's assume that my friend spent $1,500 for a mission trip to Colombia, South America. In those days that same money would have funded 6,000 meals in one of the hot lunch centers. That translated into a hot meal a day for a year for sixteen children. On the surface it is obvious the man would have done well to have stayed home and sent his money. He didn't!

Instead, he worked from daylight to dark for twelve days building tables and chairs for one of the new centers that still lacked furniture. Again, couldn't the ten tables and sixty chairs have been built by a Colombian, thus providing that person with a job? Many would argue that the man should have stayed in the U.S.A and sent his money. He didn't.

Let's look at the story as it developed over the next thirty years. We will never know if Mr. Nicks would have sent the full $1,500 plus the money he spent on materials once he arrived, had he not come.

Unpredictable spiritual experiences occur when people travel outside their comfort zones away from family and friends. Many of their defense mechanisms tumble and they become vulnerable to the movement of the Holy Spirit in their lives. When this happens, people hear God's call on their lives and make decisions that carry the potential to change them forever. Such was the case of Mr. Nicks. He found a new passion.

Volunteers on mission trips should accept the possibility they will come face to face with the reality that the world is bigger than their own country. And, such a view causes people to begin to pray, "God bless the world," and not "God bless my country;" or, "Give them their daily bread," and not "give us our daily bread." People on mission trips expand their worldview so the globe becomes more than a sphere with country names written on it. Suddenly, specific people literally walk within the outlines of specific countries. No one can estimate or underestimate the number of life-long friendships formed between people of different countries during effectively coordinated mission trips. One twenty-four hour home visit may lead to a lifetime of endless enrichment for the family units involved.

In the case of Mr. Richard Nicks, he returned to his home church of less than 100 people in Tennessee and began to promote a monthly Sunday school offering for hot lunches for the children in Colombia. Over the course of the next 25 years, he contributed and raised more than $65,000. Using the figures above, he ultimately raised the funds for 712 children to receive a hot lunch daily for a year.

Upon his death his son perpetuated his love for children by establishing an endowment that has grown to more than $53,000, providing a perpetual distribution of food for hungry kids. The figures speak: $1,500 invested for a ticket; $118,000 raised for children.

The question is still being asked, "Should you or shouldn't you go?"

Colombia 1983

"The Eye of the Tiger"

A missionary's experiences and opportunities stretch beyond expectations. The opportunities to make a difference in the lives of people in need never cease. The blessings of partnering with other cultures are multiple. Occasionally, this life of excitement takes a missionary through near-death experiences that he or she hopes not to experience again. However, people learn a lot about themselves by the way they react when face-to-face with a life and death situation.

Buenaventura, Colombia, is one of the most unattractive cities of the world; yet, one of the most interesting. The residents amaze visitors with their kindness and hospitality. Poverty dominates so much of the city. Its "emptiness" always grabbed my attention. Even though it rained two out of every three days, the trash only washed a little further down the road to a neighbor or finally into the sea where it was sequestered by the waves in inlets or washed back onto the crowded black sand beaches. The pounding rains and lack of regulations against gluing posters onto street property walls made it nearly impossible for even the most diligent property owners to keep their building looking attractive.

The heat was oppressive, with a daily high slightly above 90 °F and a humidity that hovered near 85% daily. Air-conditioning was non-existent, even in restaurants. In fact, most people not eating in their homes grabbed a quick, inexpensive snack from a street vendor who was selling the popular fried fish, *arepas*, fried chicken, steamed salted potatoes, fried or steamed *platanos*, *sancocho* (soup), *empanadas*, coffee, *aguapanela* (a drink made for brown sugar and water), and a host of other items so familiar on the coast. At night the street became a center for "hanging out" and fused music—traditional and modern sort of bubbled out of grills, bars, and even coffee shops. The absence of work and space for recreation proved a fermenting ground for alcoholism and crime. Only fortunate family homes and churches provided a safe environment from every conceivable drug, a variety of gangs, street fights, drive-by shootings, and petty-to-armed theft. An indescribable darkness prevailed over the city even in the light of day.

We picked up four mission team members from different barrios, and hurried to find the dock where we would catch our boat for the Pacific journey to the San Juan River. A thin muscular Don Antonio awaited us at one of the hundreds of tiny unstable docks sandwiched between dilapidated wooden shacks built on stilts over the sea. His thirty-foot wooden boat had lost the majority of its green and white paint due to frequent passages through sea brine. I saw a 50-gallon barrel just back of the center of the boat obviously carrying the petro we would need for a week on the river. Everyone scrambled to board our cargo since our time was limited. We had to load the boat and depart for the main channel before the tide retreated for another day.

As our boat purred away from the dock we watched young boys swimming in the heavily contaminated waters where the people in huts had thrown their trash and waste day by day. They bobbed, smiled, and waved in our small wake. Finally we reached the open sea but we were never out of the site of the gliding gulls and diving pelicans. I wondered how the pelicans kept from breaking their necks or going blind as they plummeted 100 feet straight down into the water, submerged momentarily and then surfaced with the fish they had sighted with their keen eyes from high above the sea.

After three hours of rather calm seas, we were warned that we were approaching the so-called "Eye of the Tiger." The passage from the salt water of the Pacific Ocean to the fresh water of the San Juan River would be vicious. The convergence of the two forces of water created 10 to 30 foot waves that could only be maneuvered by someone rich with experience and a dependable boat and motor. Later, we were informed that many boats had been lost at this very site. In fact, our own boat sank at the site several years after our trip.

When I felt and saw the first major wave build and rise, I was comforted; the boat easily climbed the five to eight foot swell until the bow reached skyward out of the water; then the weight and velocity of the boat pulled us forward and downward with a heavy slamming of the bottom of the boat onto the momentarily quiet sea. But then, I panicked as the next wave approached. It was at least two times higher than the previous one and had a large lip at the top slobbering toward us. The captain approached and climbed this wave less directly. It seemed like several minutes until we reached the top of the liquid mountain; I wondered if we were going to tip over and be eaten by the thrashing of one wave against another. I was thankful I had brought a life jacket, but fully aware that no one else had one. I wondered if the waves could get any more intense.

Up until that point everyone had reacted like a group of teenagers on a roller coaster. But, then, we saw what looked like the grand daddy of sea creatures. I was alarmed and glanced back to see the captain's expression; he appeared vigilant but not fearful. Suddenly, I heard the young man next to me say "Thank you, Jesus." Instantly, I wondered, *Has he gone mad?* The climb of this wave duplicated the previous except for a few moments when the small vessel inched above the top of the wave, and I couldn't see another wave. I saw nothing but the sky ahead and we began a free-fall downward much like a pelican, neatly slicing into the river. Water nearly flooded the boat, but we surfaced relieved and fully within the calm and safety of the river.

As I retraced the past few minutes, I realized that I had faced the moment of potential disaster with a definite sense of peaceful confidence that all would work out fine; the other young man saw the potential tragedy as an opportunity to thank God in all things. Both responses were based on a trust in the sovereignty of God and a faith that all things do work out for those who love the Lord and are called according to God's purposes.

Ecuador 1983

"The Pitfalls of Prosperity"

We learn the most in unexpected places and circumstances. These teachable moments can sometimes shock us into a better understanding of ourselves.

Missionaries often find it very difficult to live at the same financial level of the people they serve. I am now ashamed that our family had a much larger home, better furniture, and a newer car than any of the pastors or elders on our team!

This lesson came to me in an unexpected but powerful way. Some friends from Ecuador were national leaders who made about one dollar for every twenty dollars we were paid. We rationalized our advantages in many ways, none of which were excusable. Unbelievably, they quietly overlooked our need for the luxuries of this life. They occasionally spent holidays and other times of celebration with us. One of the most memorable times we spent together was not really a good one. They had spent a week in our home as a respite from their pastorate. It was a week of playing dominos, trips to a local pool, praying together, eating great food, and other times of joy. Sadly, an unforeseen problem developed.

Several weeks later I flew to Ecuador to visit this family at their home. Their adobe house was just a block from their church. The church dated from the earliest years of the evangelical church in Ecuador. Since my friend was not ordained, I visited him once a year to serve Holy Communion to his congregation. I arrived and was met at the door with the normal formalities—"Buenas tardes. Que tal?" He quickly warned me, "Julieta is concerned about something and needs to talk to you." I said, "What's the problem?" He said, "You better talk to her." When she saw me, she broke into tears. I asked gently, "What is wrong, Julieta?" She said, "I am so ashamed. I have sinned against you and your family. Please forgive me. While I was at your home last month, I noticed all of the bottles of deodorant in your closet. You had so many and we couldn't afford to buy one for our family, and I stole one." We had always bought many months' supply of this special brand while in the states and it was stockpiled in the guest bathroom. I was humbled. I was ashamed. I felt so selfish, so insensitive to their needs. I said, "Julieta, you don't need to ask me for forgiveness; I am the one who has sinned. Forgive me! I am so sorry I put you in that position." I don't remember what happened after that, except a flood of tears from both of us. I can say that this friendship has continued to this day...only in a much more sensitive expression of love one to another as needs and blessings occur.

U.S.A. 1990

"Respecting the Seventh Generation"

Not many people knew Rev. Claude Gilbert. He dedicated many years of his life serving as a field worker among the Choctaw Indians in southeast Oklahoma. One of his greatest contributions was a constant effort to educate people about the wisdom, dignity, and rights of the American Indian. Here is just one example from the American Indian that we all desperately need to hear!

In his book, *Spiritual Ecology*, published in 1990, Jim Nolman quotes the tremendous wisdom of the American Indian. According to the great law of the *Haudenosaunee*, the six-nation Iroquois confederacy, the leaders of the tribe respected an obligation to the needs of those who would live 150 to 200 years in the future. Their law read: "In our every deliberation we must consider the impact of our decisions on the next seven generations." This perspective is quite a contrast from the materialistic, selfish "one-generation" decisions so characteristic of contemporary politics.

Colombia 1991—2013

"The Power of Unity within the Body of the Church"

Some of us see human anomalies in creation and wonder *Why?* We continue to ask unanswerable questions, hoping we will be the one who can uncover a yet undiscovered answer to the reason for birth defects and disease. A more productive way to confront the unfortunate situation of others or ourselves is to react with compassion to a bad situation in the best way we can. When many people focus on doing what they can, significant strides toward a better life can be made.

Let me tell you about Jose Bravo. Jose was born in a one-room thatch hut on the bank of a jungle river near Guapi, Colombia. Guapi is a coastal Pacific village where former African slaves of the Spanish colonists have dwelled for more than 100 years. Life has been day-to-day for most of them. Jose was born with a partial nose, no upper lip, no teeth. His eyes rested further apart than normal, with restricted vision. His birth defect left no way to eat except to receive liquids through an eyedropper or spoon.

Can you imagine the feelings of the family when they saw this little baby? They were overwhelmed with fear as to whether or not the baby would survive. The mother suffered from a serious learning disability that barely allowed her to carry on a conversation, but totally unable to learn more than the skills qualifying her for menial tasks. It is questionable whether she fully understood the extreme health problems of her baby. What she didn't know was that a string of acts of love and compassion would be offered her son that would provide a magnificent change for her baby and also reveal the glory of God. Sadly, this would require the decision to allow her child to live his childhood in another country and eventually to be adopted. However, without that sacrifice, Jose could not have the surgeries needed for him to see and speak.

Many times God brings people together through what many people call providence. It is as if God requests a particular task from a variety of people in order to accomplish a purpose that is larger than what any one person can accomplish. And, when all of those people respond by doing their part, a shift in destiny can occur.

The little boy was referred to a Colombian social worker while she was on a mission trip to the small village. She secured permission from the mother to take the baby with her to Cali for an evaluation. Anyone who knew the compassionate social worker understood that she would find a way to make things happen with the least money anyone could imagine. The Cali doctors found the defects so extreme they couldn't help in any substantial way.

A missionary saw Jose during his visit to Cali and began to look for options for the infant. Soon thereafter, this missionary met a "Project Smile" doctor on a plane. He was a part of a team of surgeons who do plastic facial surgery without a fee in third world countries. The doctor saw Jose during a visit to Cali and felt he would have to live in the U.S.A. for a period of several years and receive multiple surgeries. Jose was escorted from Cali to New Orleans, where an American family agreed to serve as his foster parents. This decision implied more sacrifice of time and energy than they could have imagined. But, they say, "Jose has been one of the greatest blessings our family could have received."

Approximately three years into the surgeries the host family brought four-year-old Jose to Memphis for me to meet. When I picked him up, he gave me a big kiss on the lips with his newly constructed lip, a feat he could never have done three years earlier.

More than twenty years have passed; teams of volunteer surgeons have operated on Jose 32 times to reconstruct his face and to adjust for the growth that has come yearly to his body. Jose, now adopted by his U.S.A. family, copes with learning disabilities, speech difficulties, and limited vision. His determination is amazing. He has performed with the Red Hot Brass Band at Carnegie Hall and on NPR radio. These days, fewer people ask "Why?" concerning Jose than when he was born. Today, his smile is widely known in New Orleans and God's name has been glorified with each step of progress.

We underestimate the role that God has in mind for us on any given day. We have learned by observation that when God's people work together they accomplish much more than when they labor alone.

China 1991

"The Impossible Made Tangible"

Do you remember an individual's experience that can be documented, but appears too incredible to be true? The following story of God's protection of a faithful believer caused me to blink several times in amazement. I traveled to Mainland China for the first time in 1991. We visited the Sha Kai Three Self Patriotic Church near Zongshan, just across the Pearl River Delta from Hong Kong. This little church was a Cumberland Presbyterian congregation prior to the Cultural Revolution (1966-1976) when all religion was prohibited during the leadership of Mao Zedong. During that decade Sha Kai church was closed and converted to a factory. Following Mao's death in 1976, the Chinese government relaxed their persecution of religion and began to return some church properties to the Three Self Patriotic Church. Sha Kai was one of the properties recovered and reopened. Gradually, members of the original congregation returned to worship.

During our discussions with the pastor of Sha Kai, we secured permission to meet some of the older leaders of the church who had lived through the Japanese invasion of China and the Cultural Revolution. The pastor guided us on a fifteen-minute walk to the home of Elder Song, a writer and the principal leader of the congregation prior to 1966. People stopped to gaze as we made our way around street vendors and lazy dogs sleeping on the sidewalk. As the streets narrowed and sidewalks disappeared, we made a sharp turn onto a dirt path. The path ended on the stoop of a small one-story whitewashed adobe house. Red petunias hung in a planter just above a bronze bell used to signal the arrival of a guest.

A slender lady opened the door and the pastor explained the purpose of our visit. We were led to a small patio that faced out to more bamboo. The house was obviously the last one on the hillside, which dropped quickly toward the valley below. The birds sang happily. And, occasionally some of the smaller song birds would swoop into a nearby feeder.

Our hostess said her husband was aware of our arrival and that he would soon come to speak with us. A younger woman walked by his side as his slippers scraped along the titled floor. His smile welcomed us without a word. He slowly eased into a wooden straight-back chair in front of us. Only, then did he speak softly, "I am honored to have you visit my humble home."

His wife did most of the talking for her husband, sharing that Elder Song was thankful to live to the age of 83. During an hour visit we expressed our interest in how they survived during the years Christians were harshly persecuted. She related that ill treatment began quickly when Mao announced his decision to close churches and deny everyone the freedom of religion. Government officials forced their way into both churches and homes to confiscate all Bibles, religious literature, crosses, or visual representations of Christ or the church.

The key leaders of each church received the most severe persecution to strike fear into others. Any efforts to violate the edicts of the government resulted in beatings and imprisonment. The severe actions intended to cleanse the society of any Western influence or loyalties that interfered with commitments to Communist dogma. The strongest leaders of churches were selected for reorientation camps. Elder Song was one scheduled for such a penalty. The camps included months of brainwashing and oppressive labor. However, just a few days prior to his departure, a stroke paralyzed him from the neck down. He was unable to leave his bed for more than a decade, requiring the full-time care of his wife. He remained faithful through all of those years, teaching and witnessing in the privacy of his home. Following the death of Mao and the government's increased leniency to religion, Elder Song recovered the use of his body and his health was largely restored.

I often remember this story when my life or the life of those I love appears overwhelming. A believer needs never rule out the possibility of a miracle even when it arrives dressed in a way we might not expect or desire. God confirms his promise to walk side-by-side with us even through the valley of the shadow of death. We sometimes witness the unthinkable when God is involved—I felt the impossible became tangible in the testimony of Elder Song.

Africa 1991

"Just Getting There and Home Is a Mission in Itself"

Missionaries should be seen as air warriors. Few people realize the stress of just getting to and from the country of their assignments. I would define an air warrior not by miles flown but by the combat endured. The sometime dangers of international travel aren't a part of a missionary's job description.

One such extended battle began in New York City when I boarded an international flight to Abidjan, Ivory Coast on Air Afrique. Sometimes you get a sense about what will follow by how it begins. We sat grounded by fog for three hours before take off.

Thirteen hours later we landed in Dakar, Senegal for fuel and more passengers. The agent booked us through Senegal and the Ivory

Coast because there were no direct flights to Monrovia, Liberia. We were some of the first people to visit the country during the brief period of peace enforced by the Economic Community of West African States Monitoring Group. A church colleague, Joe Snider, and I made the journey to encourage Liberian Christians and to review how we could best help in the country's rehabilitation efforts.

Our stay in Abidjan, Ivory Coast, included the amenity that we would be rewarded at nearly every stop both going and coming—a delay. The layover grew from four to eight hours, pushing back our arrival in Conakry, Guinea, to midnight.

The Guinea airport resembled a sidewalk sale with one hundred customers looking for the same bargain in front of one table. Two scrappy sweating teenagers grabbed our bags and shouted something in French. We walked briskly as they led us through a maze of customs, immigration, health checks, and dispatch. Our self-appointed helpers then tossed our bags into the trunk of a taxi in the dimly lit parking zone, and held up a sign in English, "$20 please." My friend knew that was way too high from his previous flights in Africa and gave them $5. The guys were not happy and undoubtedly cast a few French curses our way as we crawled into the dilapidated taxi and slammed the door. We handed our hotel address to the driver, and he nodded, smiled, and mumbled, "I know. We go."

Within a minute we left civilization and entered a freaky darkness of a twilight zone. It took an eternal ten minutes before we would see another vehicle or a light. I looked toward Joe periodically and he sat like a stoic monk, evidently not as concerned as I. I finally whispered, "Could this guy be taking us somewhere to jump, kill, and rob us?" He just smiled and said, "You worry too much."

We finally arrived at the tiny hotel where a simple card table served for check in. Again, the driver requested $30 and we decided to give him $15. He kept badgering us through our registration and started to follow us to our room until the attendant turned him back.

This would be a short night because of our 8 a.m. departure. The next morning we spoke with another traveler and learned the taxi fare to or from the airport was $8. When we arrived at the airport the baggage boys converged upon us like ducks looking for a piece of bread. Finally two guys won the screaming contest, grabbed our bags and pulled us toward their pre-determined path. It was scary to lose complete control of our possessions and our movement through the airport. We went behind the airline counter, through a filthy employee break room, and onto the airfield. The one visible plane belonged to a different airline.

We soon learned that our particular plane didn't fly on Friday. Our agent had not done due diligence in researching African airlines. So, there we were, looking for another taxi back to the city with no way to contact our Liberian hosts about the change in arrival dates.

The next morning we were negotiating again with the taxi driver because of our early departure; he insisted that the price doubled. I began formulating in my mind a presentation to mail to Guinness to nominate Conakry as the most difficult airport in the world.

This time the baggage boys ignored us and we pushed our way through the throng of people to the miniature airport check-in. We reverted to the early days of international aviation—no computers, no respect for lines, and no nothing. We had fallen right into the center of chaos and the French language. We literally shoved our way toward the counter as others tried to make end runs around us. I used my suitcase to block the flow on my right while Joe's bulk slowed the other side. People warned us that smaller airlines often sold unlimited tickets for limited seating; the seats were given to the fastest and the strongest. Somehow, we managed to get our tickets approved and then faced the expected bribe for the custom's officer as well as the departure tax. All of this required francs. Fortunately, we had enough of the currency to pay these fees because it was obvious there was no monetary exchange service in the airport. We met "Zacchaeus" at the last desk before leaving for the plane. He insisted on seeing our billfolds to check for Guinea currency. He was firm that no Guinea money could leave the country. He confiscated the last few bills and coins we had. We were glad to toss that money into his pot to exit the country.

When we climbed the wobbly rusted steps, I could see we would be flying on a small World War II aircraft. The well-appointed aircraft included no life jackets, no inflight service, no seatbelts, and no escape orientation. A couple of caps over the oxygen ports were totally missing. I was thankful there were two people in the front seats, so I assumed we at least had two pilots. One half of the passenger seats were removed to clear space for baggage and cargo. It would be misleading to say we had no flight attendant. There was a lady who stood at the entrance of the plane to check our tickets, and then disappeared until she came back with coffee for herself and sat down never to move again.

This was my first time to travel with baggage that moved around, made disgruntled sounds, and even stunk up the place. Not only were we hauling local beer, boxes of fruit and vegetables, but we also had two white bearded goats, one plump pig ready for market, and several crates of restless white and red chickens. Wouldn't you know I sat next to one of the goats that kept trying to nibble on my pant leg? The brief flight could not end quickly enough.

We arrived in Monrovia 24 hours late and unannounced. Since Jimmy Carter was also arriving for peace meetings, the tiny airport was buzzing with people. Our hosts were not at the airport to receive us.

We cleared baggage claim, immigration, and customs—it was so good to hear English again, even if the accent was heavy and difficult to understand. I learned the importance of having a travel mate in the third world; one person could watch the luggage while the other did necessary paper work and handled all negotiation.

Once again, we found ourselves at the mercy of the taxi driver. We explained we were on a mission trip and he proceeded to charge us three times the normal cost.

(Note: Our visit in Liberia was ten days of unbelievable exposure to sadness and despair. We did our best to bring some hope, but we left with a feeling the peace initiative would not last. And, it didn't. But, this story only tells the difficulties of air travel.)

When we tried to confirm our flight to Abidjan to leave Liberia, agents told us the flight had been cancelled. Their next flight was four days later—just what I wanted, four more days in a country teetering on the edge of war and swarming with soldiers. So, instead we purchased tickets on Weasua Airlines. I always get concerned when I can't even pronounce the name of the airlines.

When we arrived the following day to catch our flight, Amos Sawyer, the acting President of Liberia, needed our plane to return from a peace conference in Yamoussoukro, the capital of the Ivory Coast and that we would not be able to fly directly to Abidjan. Instead, they suggested we fly to Yamoussoukro on the plane going to retrieve the President, and then rent a taxi for $30 for the three-hour drive across the Ivory Coast to Abidjan. That was the only immediate option and we agreed with little thought. I just wanted to head for home.

Upon arrival in Yamoussoukro, the place was humming with officials, African drummers, bands, young enthusiastic dancers in bright orange and red costumes, and adequate security to dispatch all the presidents of West African countries departing from the peace conference. When we deplaned, we ran into a significant obstacle. No one told us we needed a visa for land travel across the Ivory Coast. And, we were only getting portions of the bad news in a mixture of French and English. Finally, we found a bi-lingual Peace Corps worker when we heard him swear in English. He agreed to negotiate with officials about the visa and eventually secured a one-day pass for our travel. Then, when we found a taxi, we were shocked to find out that the taxi was not the estimated $30, but $300. Such a fee was out of our range of possibility. Eventually, we booked a bus for the three and a half hour ride to Abidjan for about $25, hoping we could catch our late evening flight. It was a very bumpy ride on cushion-less seats. The upside was the blaring Bruce Lee video heavily laced with violence and sexual espionage.

After an additional 24-hour delay in Abidjan, we were able to confirm a flight back to New York. I stopped at the top of the steps before entering the plane and turned my head for one last look at the so-called "dark continent." This road warrior was returning exhausted, but unscathed physically, from the battle. But, I also remembered somewhere a host of other missionaries were just trying to get to the location of their work to face challenges beyond their expectations.

China 1991

"Blood-Stained Glory"

"In fact, the law requires that nearly everything be cleansed with blood, and without the shedding of blood there is no forgiveness. Just as people are destined to die once, and after that to face judgment, so Christ was sacrificed once to take away the sins of many; and he will appear a second time, not to bear sin, but to bring salvation to those who are waiting for him" (Hebrews 9:22, 27-28).

It isn't possible to relate some experiences with the intensity or emotion they deserve. How can you capture with words the sacrifice people make to secure religious and political freedom?

The incredible history and culture of China dwelled behind dense clouds of mystery for centuries. The average non-Chinese only imagined the beauty and mystic of the Great Wall, the Forbidden City, or the Terra Cotta Soldiers. Even Chinese citizens knew little about their country. Then, Deng Xiaoping (1904-1997), a leader from the peasant class, rose to power with Mao Zedong. After Mao's death, he led China through the first stages of a market reform that opened some doors to the West while continuing to severely restrict the religious and personal freedoms of his people.

But, the crack for foreigners was wide enough for me to visit a few churches in Mainland China in 1991. My second stop after visiting a church in Sha Kai was Guangzhou (formerly Canton) in hopes of finding the gravesite of Rev. Gam Sing Quah. Rev. Quah, a young convert living in the U.S.A., came under a deep personal conviction to plant Cumberland Presbyterian churches in China. He set sail from San Francisco on October 8, 1908 as an employee of the Women's Board of Missions of the Cumberland Presbyterian Church. By 1923 he had organized eight churches. He died in 1937 in Canton, leaving the ministry to his two sons—Samuel and McAdoo.

While in Guangzhou my guide and I toured the impressive Sun Yat Sin Memorial. Sun Yat Sin was the founding father of the Republic of China. As we sat in the nearly vacant auditorium, I noticed my guide become quiet as we listened to the music being played quietly over the sound system. The tune was captivating even though I could not understand a single word. We must have sat fifteen minutes or more listening to the mystical music. When I glanced at my host, tears were gently flowing down her cheeks. So, I sat and assumed this was a special moment. Finally, she said, "You know, I am really surprised with this music. "Blood-Stained Glory" is the name of the song. Students listened to it for inspiration in the Tiananmen Square in Beijing before the government massacre two years ago. It's hard to believe the government would allow it played here at this time in our history." Later, I would learn the lyrics of "Blood-Stained Glory" tell the story of the price paid for freedom, regardless of the country.

"Perhaps I'll bid farewell and never to return, can you comprehend? Do you understand?

Perhaps I will fall and never to rise again. Will you be forever waiting?

If it's to be so, grieve not, the flag of our Republic has our blood-stained glory.

If it's to be so, grieve not, the flag of our Republic has our blood-stained glory.

Perhaps my eyes will shut and never open again, will you understand my silent emotions?

Perhaps I will sleep forever, never able to wake up.

Will you believe that I have been transformed into mountains?

If it's to be so, grieve not, the soil of our Republic contains the love we have given.

If it's to be so, grieve not, the soil of our Republic contains the love we have given."[3]

I sat in silence long after my host left the memorial. I felt strangely close to a people's struggle. Mental images of a young man standing in front of an approaching caravan of armed tanks passed through my mind. Few people who saw that display of bravery in Tiananmen Square will forget those moments of tension. After the young man momentarily stopped the tank, he disappeared into the crowd; to this day no one knows his identity, although some believe he was arrested and killed. The facts remain unclear.

I could not imagine at the time how critical the Tiananmen Square would be in opening China to the world. Unfortunately, there are no reliable figures to demonstrate the growth of Christianity in China since 1989, but everyone agrees that numbers have grown significantly. The lives lost in Tiananmen Square were not in vain. There are still many steps to be taken for full religious freedom to exist in China, but the wall has been knocked down and spiritual liberty is sneaking in day by day.

As I reflect politically, many people have shed blood in every nation on earth in an effort to secure freedom. No one should underestimate such cost.

But thinking theologically, only the death and spilled blood of the Lord Jesus Christ has the potential to save every person on the globe from remaining estranged from God. Oh, that everyone would be given the opportunity to receive the gift of eternal life. And, so, the incredible need for missions.

U.S.A. 1993

"A Mission Challenge"

People and God always respond dramatically when spiritual gifts are involved. Scriptures assure believers that God endows each believer with at least one spiritual gift (1 Corinthians 12:7). One of those gifts is giving (Romans 12). Generous Christians are usually those who have received that gift.

Large challenges bring out the best in people. It can be argued that we ask God for too little when it comes to matters of faith and unattainable expectations. God's power to meet legitimate needs exceeds everyone's hope. On occasions, we receive not because we ask not. "You do not have because you do not ask God. When you ask, you do not receive, because you ask with wrong motives, that you may spend what you get on your pleasures" (James 4:2*b*-3).

A significant change occurred in my life in 1991. The Executive Director of the Mission Board of our denomination offered me the position of Director of Global Missions. I felt like the job was right for my skill-set and my interest in missionaries and developing a global church.

Part of my responsibility as a mission executive was fundraising. For the first time in recent history, our denominational missionaries would be required to raise their own salaries (deputation). The Dyersburg Cumberland Presbyterian Church was approached about the possibility of giving monthly toward the financial support of an individual missionary. The pastor was open to the idea and invited me to consult with their mission committee about this possibility. I explained to the committee that missionaries were now responsible to raise their support package and that if a church contributed to such support, it could consider that missionary as a part of its church staff. This would signal to their congregation and to the community the congregation's commitment to comply in obedience with the Great Commission found in Matthew 28:16-20.

"Then the eleven disciples went to Galilee, to the mountain where Jesus had told them to go. When they saw him, they worshiped him;

but some doubted. Then Jesus came to them and said, 'All authority in heaven and on earth has been given to me. Therefore go and make disciples of all nations, baptizing them in the name of the Father and of the Son and of the Holy Spirit, and teaching them to obey everything I have commanded you. And surely I am with you always, to the very end of the age.'"

The committee was excited and recommended consideration of the program to their session. The following month I met with the session to answer their questions. We discussed presenting the program to the entire church. So, I returned later to challenge a group of 150 people in their fellowship hall. The request was simple. Would the congregation support an ongoing monthly contribution to fund part of the salary of missionaries Boyce and Beth Wallace?

Following the presentation one person asked, "How much do you think a church our size should contribute?" This question caught me by surprise. I stood quietly and then said with uneasiness and a mustard seed-sized faith, "Well, if you start next month in July, I think you could give $1,000 a month annually. This will translate into $6,000 for the rest of the year and then you can build $12,000 into your budget for future years." One member immediately stood and said, "I can give $1,000." Another gentleman quickly said, "I will also give $1,000." And, just as quickly a third popped up, smiled, and said, "I will give the other 4,000!" I was stunned.

In a matter of three minutes, we had raised the entire request from three people. The other 147 people sat speechless without an opportunity to make a commitment. After processing what had happened, I quipped, "My goodness, I wish I had asked for $50,000," and everyone burst into laughter.

Twenty years later in 2013, the Dyersburg congregation's commitment has grown to $14,000 annually for the support of a missionary family. That one request, made with a bit of trepidation, has yielded more than a $250,000 for missions. It all began when three men manifested the spiritual gift of giving.

Part of the responsibility of a mission leader is challenging one's church to give at a level higher than believed attainable. Only then, will the people respond to their potential.

Macau 1993

"The Gift of Hospitality"

A young Chinese woman sitting across the table during our orientation session grabbed my attention. She was obviously a church leader, her smile and overall countenance reminded me of my conception of an angel. I felt compelled to speak personally with her at the end of our meeting.

With the assistance of an interpreter, I spoke, "Please forgive me, but I am so curious. Your peaceful smile obviously reflects a relationship with God! Would it be possible for you to share with me about your faith?" Her testimony left me deeply touched and reconfirmed my belief in the personal nature of God.

"My husband and I have only recently become Christians. We grew up in Buddhist families. After we were married, my mother-in-law stressed the need to worship numerous idols and to go through the daily rituals of ancestor worship. Since my husband and I lived with the family and I was the youngest woman, it became my responsibility to complete these religious chores. I began to act more religious, but the whole routine meant little to me personally.

Then tragedy crashed down on our family. I don't remember the doctor's words. I simply recall the sense of nausea, a deep emptiness, and a weakness that engulfed my whole body upon learning that my husband had cancer. The doctor felt it might be treatable if we were able to secure the proper care in Hong Kong, but living in Macau and having limited finances made that very difficult. We began to recall family members who lived in Hong Kong. We telephoned each one of them to see if it would be possible for us to come and live with them for a few months during the time of my husband's surgery, treatment, and recovery. Every call resulted in disappointment. Our relatives either had no room or some other reason why they could not receive us as their houseguests. Finally, we remembered our distant cousins, Helen and Luke. When we called their home, their response lifted our spirits—"Yes, we would be glad to receive you as our guests during this time."

Our family warned us that these relatives were Christian, but what were we supposed to do? My husband's parents worried that if we omitted the ancestor worship and adoration of the house idols, their son wouldn't be healed. But the Cheung's seemed to be the only alternative. So we moved in for our extended visit in Luke and Helen's home. My husband received surgery and extensive chemotherapy, and for the next two months we stayed in the home of Luke and Helen.

The home atmosphere differed considerably. There were no altars to ancestors. The dependence upon fortune-telling to try to determine the future simply didn't enter into their minds. Instead, their religion merged every day with life and decisions in a coherent and logical manner. The Cheung's faith affected their attitudes and their ethics. Gradually, Luke and Helen began to ask if we would like to share in their time of Bible study together. Gently, they began to pray with us. They offered to pray for the healing of my husband, and somehow we noticed a vitality and faith we had never seen before. More important than the verbalization of their faith was the love they showed to us each day that we spent in their home. They understood our pain and sympathized with our anxiety. They shared in the responsibility of caring that resulted from our suffering. We began to feel closer to them than to our own family. Throughout the entire illness, they suggested that not only was the medical treatment we were receiving important but that we needed to place our trust in the Great Physician, Jesus Christ. The treatment of my husband was successful, and now the doctors can find no traces of cancer. Since that time, we've returned to our home, but our memories of Luke and Helen's hospitality, their love, their concern, and their deep faith have not left our minds. Several months after we returned to Macau, we began to attend the Christian church and made the decision to accept Jesus Christ as the Lord and Savior of our lives.

We've learned many things we didn't know before that time. We now know that the Bible does witness that Jesus healed people of every disease and sickness (Matthew 9:35). We have captured the impact of the love chapter of the Bible (1 Corinthians 13). We understand by reading Hebrews 11 that faith is an imperative part of the Christian faith. And we've come to understand the importance of the gift of the Holy Spirit in each believer's life. Our church has taught us that evangelism is a Christian responsibility. We realize as we reflect about our conversion, that it was through one of the gifts of the Holy Spirit—the gift of hospitality (Romans 12:13)—that Luke and Helen could most effectively evangelize us and help us to see the validity of Christianity.

We praise God for his wonderful grace. We are beginning to pray and ask that he will show us the gift he has given to us so that we can use it to lead others to him."

Japan 1995

"Giving Back"

"Giving back" is an inspirational and practical concept. It allows individuals or institutions to "regift" what they have received, thus allowing a gift to keep on giving well into the future.

Years ago the Cumberland Presbyterian Denomination provided part of the money for the purchase of land for the Kunitachi-Nozomi congregation in Japan. That congregation didn't forget the importance of such an example to help birth another church. When the Kunitachi Church paid off its remaining debt for their church building, they made a very unselfish decision. They transferred the $20,000 allotted annually for debt reduction to a line item for church planting and began to give that money annually to the Megumi Church Fellowship to assist with their needs as a new church.

A church finally freed from debt might have been tempted to buy a new organ, put away money for a rainy day, or add another staff person; instead they chose to invest in the birth of a new church.

The early Christian church was known for its generous sharing of possessions one with another. Acts 2:44-45 records "All the believers were together and had everything in common. They sold property and possessions to give to anyone who had need."

Russian Republics 1995

"Using the Cultural Decorum for Faith Purposes"

God's methods to work his ultimate will are astounding. Sometimes God achieves his purposes quickly, but more often it occurs over years, decades, or lifetimes. We need to remember that chronological time is much less important to God than to us. God works in the framework of an eternity and we constantly have a stopwatch in our hand.

Years ago, I was flying to visit missionaries in a predominately Muslim country in Asia. That nation was categorized by missiologists as a "closed" country—one where the gospel could not be preached openly, so I traveled as a tourist rather than a mission executive.

When I sent my itinerary to the missionaries, they responded that one of their converts would be on the same plane. We met in Los Angeles and made arrangements to sit side-by-side; I learned that his parents were troubled by his conversion and banned the missionaries from their home. We often forget that in countries where none or few people have converted to Christianity, new believers are persecuted in a myriad of ways. Some are disinherited. Others are beaten. They lose their jobs. Their businesses are boycotted. In the most extreme cases some are martyred. The temporal blessings of the gift of salvation often have a very high price.

In this particular case, the convert was threatened and ignored by family and community for a period of months, but was finally able to return and enjoy his parent's love. However, the family wanted nothing to do with Christianity or its representatives.

After getting acquainted, the conversation shifted to faith and family. He said, "I would like for you to meet my parents."

I said, "Do you think they would be open to that? I would certainly enjoy the opportunity."

He smiled and said, "In our culture, when a stranger appears at your door with a family member, you are more or less required to invite him for tea."

The missionaries picked us up at the airport. They delivered him to his home. His parents were elated to see their son after two years of college in the U.S.A. They not only invited me for tea, but also asked the missionaries to enter. The reception was warmer than we could have hoped.

This positive experience led to an invitation for the missionaries and me to visit their farm in the country. What a blessing! This unique cultural expectation led to the reconciliation of the missionaries and the Moslem family.

The natural follow-up question is: What is God's will for this family? The rest of that story is yet to be written. Our faith leads us to find hope in the mantra—"Whosoever Will May Come."

Colombia 2000

"God Spoke Very Loudly Here"

Colombia was shaken with a strong earthquake in 1999 that left more than 60% of the city of Armenia in rubble. The 300 members of one church were significantly affected with more than 30 families losing their homes. Many churches responded in various ways, including the recruitment of twelve teams to help with reconstruction efforts.

I was one of the team leaders and decided to invite two of my sons, David and Steven, to join the teams along with their wives, Victoria and Jenny. Both of my sons had spent a portion of their childhood in Colombia as missionary kids, so I suspected they would want to assist with this crisis. Steve and Jenny were quick to respond positively. David was much more reserved about the whole thing. He waited until the last minute to commit to the trip. I was a bit confused by the whole delay because David is usually quick to respond to anything that has to do with assisting a neighbor in need.

Upon arriving in Armenia we met with the Colombia leadership for orientation. They had our ten-day stay well-planned. It involved construction work, coffee farm visits, shopping, interaction with Colombian brothers and sisters, and worship.

David and I were the only bi-lingual members of our team since Steven was too young when he left the country to retain his Spanish. So, the Armenia church asked David and me to participate in the Sunday worship. I was to preach and they asked David to give a testimony about his personal walk with God. I immediately began to wonder what he would say since I knew that he had gotten rather inattentive to his spiritual life during his college years. He had continued to attend church on an infrequent basis, but was sort of avoiding the strong commitment that he had been taught to be of high importance.

The week was filled with blood, sweat, and tears. Even though Armenia had begun to rebound from the loss of property and loved ones, little clues of destruction lurked around every corner. Family pictures blew through the work place with every passing wind. There was still a smell of destruction and death in some areas of the city. The fragility of life was written in invisible letters everywhere you looked. Tent cities occupied numerous areas of the city, mostly in parks or vacant lots. People were worshipping in the open air since some sanctuaries now looked as if they had been bombed in a time of war. Our host pastor had converted his home into a feeding station and a warehouse for food that was being sent or brought from caring people around Colombia and the world. The compassionate response from the world wrote contemporary stories of "good Samaritans."

My mind would occasionally drift to the irony that David had been asked to share his testimony in this city in the midst of transition and pain. I wondered what he would have to share and how effective he would be at communicating after so long without using Spanish.

The service was one of those times when there was no doubt that the Holy Spirit had plans. The attendees arrived highly alert for worship. They had come to hear what God might say during this time and situation. I have no idea what I preached that Sunday, but I do remember David's testimony almost word-for-word. Part of that was because he is my son and I care deeply about his relationship with God.

David began, "You know, when Dad asked me to join the team to Colombia, I didn't want to come. My reluctance was not because I was afraid I would be kidnapped. I was not afraid I would be robbed. I wasn't even afraid I would get sick. *I didn't want to come to Colombia because I remember how loudly God spoke here.*"

He continued, "I have been very self-centered the last few years of my life. I have done what I wanted to do. I have been running on auto-pilot, rather than letting God direct my life. And God has been speaking to me everywhere I have gone. He is there when I look at the people. He is there in our devotionals. He is there in the faces of the people needing help. He is there when I go to bed and when I awake. I realize I need to make some serious changes in my life. I have not been living how God wants. I need to make some changes."

Once again I was reminded how our defense mechanisms against listening to God's call upon our lives tumble down when we leave our daily routine and the familiarity of our culture.

Colombia 2000

"A Friend Sent Me"

The little silver cross lay innocently on the carefully ironed shirts returned by the laundry lady. She announced, "I found it in the pocket of one of the pants when I scrubbed them." She was an honest person and wanted everyone to know she returned everything found in the clothes she washed.

But the next week another cross was in the laundry. The lady was inquisitive. "It has words on it in English. What do they mean?"

"It says 'Jesus is Lord,'" I said.

"Umm. It belongs to the foreigners who are here with you, doesn't it? What are they doing here?" She questioned.

"They're helping repair and rebuild houses and churches damaged in the earthquake."

"*Ave Maria!* (Good heavens!) And they came all the way here for that? Why?" She was amazed.

"Because they believe those words on the little cross, and they feel that Jesus asked them to come help people in need."

Would it be okay if I kept this cross?" She asked.

"Yes, I think someone wanted you to have it," I replied.

Curiosity lounged in doorways, hung over balconies, peeped out windows, and invented seven or eight errands a day just to see the strangers. Most of the adults were too reserved to ask questions at first, but the children had no such reserve. They gaped open-mouthed at the size of some of the visitors, laughed at sleight-of-hand tricks with pennies and endlessly tried out their limited English. These Christians were "very much good, OK!"

Many Colombian adults marveled that men and women of all ages labored at ordinary tasks for someone else, and were even willing to share their food. The translator with the group gave them New Testaments and explained what gave meaning to this humanitarian effort. Finally some of the adults lost their shyness and started asking questions through the interpreters. "Where are these people from? Why are they here?" One neighbor got up her courage and boldly stopped another translator together with one of the visitors. "They say in the neighborhood you're building another house for Alicia because hers fell down in the earthquake! And you're from another country! Why on earth would anyone come all the way here just to build a house for someone they don't even know?"

The interpreter answered: "Well, we have a Friend and He sent us."[5]

Brazil 2004

"On a Rock in a Hard Spot"

Have you ever wondered, *Where are you, God, when I need you?* Maybe God responds, "I was there; why didn't you see me?" I traveled to Brazil in 2004 to encourage missionaries and study ways to expand their ministry. It never entered my mind that the visit could be the last trip of my life. The week of Bible studies, visits to homes, prayer, and worship services filled me with optimism. My host asked me on the last day of the visit if there was anything that I would like to do for enjoyment. We had driven by the appealing Atlantic beaches on various days. So, I said, "I'd love to go for a swim and have some seafood at the beach."

My friend didn't swim, but was more than willing to eat lunch at the shore. Unfortunately, he had no idea the beach he chose was one of the most dangerous along the Bahia of Brazil.

I wandered into the water taking little notice of the undertow or the moderate waves slapping the beach every few seconds. Slowly, but surely, I walked farther and farther from the beach, careful never to allow the waves to break above my chest. All of a sudden the bottom fell out of the beach and I could no longer touch anything but the hollow ocean. This change didn't overly concern me because I planned to body surf back to the beach. I had done that in many oceans around the world. But these waves proved different, radically different! Every time I tried to ride a wave, it approached the beach and then a rip current sucked me under the water and carried me back out into the ocean to a point where I had caught the wave. My friend, comfortable under a palm tree with his coconut drink and a book, didn't realize I was in trouble. I made several unsuccessful attempts to swim toward the beach and beyond the undertow, but every endeavor resulted in a growing awareness of my weakness and the ocean's power. Finally, I was totally exhausted and choking from the ingested water. As the wave carried me in and began to pull me downward, I felt a sharp rock under my foot. My head was briefly above water. This gave me time to catch my breath and expel the water in my lungs, throat and mouth. This brief respite gave me a moment to regain my senses. I knew I had one last chance to make it to the beach. I pushed off the rock and swam for my life, taking strokes until I could not take another. When I tried to stand up, the sand was under my feet and my head was out of the water. I stumbled to the dry beach. My legs would barely support me.

Soon thereafter, I reflected about the experience. Psalm 40 came to mind, "I waited patiently for the Lord; he turned to me and heard my cry. He lifted me out of the slimy pit, out of the mud and mire; he set my feet on a rock and gave me a firm place to stand. He put a new song in my mouth, a hymn of praise to our God. Many will see and fear the Lord and put their trust in him" (Psalm 40:1-3).

I did not pray during the event. I didn't think about God. Was God aware that one of his children was drowning? Did God put the rock under my foot? Did God move me to where there was a rock? What do you think? Was this a coincidence? Does God interact with people in these and other kinds of experiences? The discussion of these kinds of questions is the first step in discovering the impact of a personal God, and people respond differently. But such questions deserve consideration.

I believe these types of experiences with God exist in everyone's life. But many people have not learned to recognize such activity of God in their lives. Others are embarrassed to talk about the times when they felt God personally visited them. And this lack of appreciation for the mighty acts of God in lives of people leads to a perception that God is distant, indifferent, and impersonal. Hence, spiritual realities slip into the unobserved and unspoken. But, God has not changed. God's nature of love and communication never changes. To coin a phrase, God is "omni-interested." God is interested in a personal relationship with everyone. Our spirituality depends on our discovery of the interest of God in forming a friendship with us. As we slowly learn to speak to God and sense an answer through the reading scripture, pausing for moments of silence, and being instructed by preaching and teaching, God becomes real and alive.

Myanmar 2004

"On the Roads of Mandalay"

I have visited orphanages around the world; they always drive my emotion to an unattainable wish to adopt the whole lot of smiling, begging faces. These love-starved children usually try to make eye contact while silently crying, "Please pick me." And, I always leave wondering why the world can't do a better job of matching lonely homeless children with desiring adults.

God has always urged us to be compassionate with widows and orphans. "Religion that God our Father accepts as pure and faultless is this: to look after orphans and widows in their distress and to keep oneself from being polluted by the world" (James 1:27).

We touched down in Yangon, Myanmar in early 2004 with representatives from World Vision International. Our goal was to visit some of the sites where monetary gifts collected through the Love Loaf Program had been distributed. These ministries included an AIDS support group, a grade school administered by Buddhist monks, a community-directed small business loan cooperative, and an orphanage. Each visit introduced us to unimagined needs.

As we walked the dusty dirt streets of Yangon, we passed small, unpainted wooden homes on stilts that backed up to the black waters carrying sewage to small canals that run throughout the slums. These canals are the only option for the removal of sewage when people move onto undeveloped land and the government is unwilling to install proper public services. Unfortunately, these moves are always the result of choosing between two miserable options. People leave a meager farm life to wiggle through the hellish tunnel of poverty while trying to find a job and some kind of makeshift lodging. The transition is never easy and for many it means sleeping on the street under a cardboard box and pilfering through the stinking garbage dumps for something to eat. We walked by a lot of people who were balancing very heavy loads on their heads. I wondered how they could bear the burden, but they smiled and moved along chatting with other Burmese they meet.

Myanmar is often called the "Land of the Pagodas," but the white or gilded golden structures are absent in the poor communities.

Our guides ushered us through the large swinging metal doors of a building resembling a small abandoned warehouse. The outside of the building had obviously been whitewashed years ago and now carried what I assumed was the graffiti of area gangs. Inside, thirty orphan boys and one smiling girl converged upon us with few inhibitions. The orphanage director tried to restrain the children, but within a few minutes they were hanging on our legs and trying to converse with us in their limited English. I was ashamed that I had not bothered even to learn the simplest greeting in Burmese.

We were privileged to take a seat on little wooden chairs from the mess hall so we could divvy out the stuffed animals, key chains, baseball caps, pens and a host of other things that we had brought as gifts. None of the kids were disappointed by their presents, but it was obvious that they constantly glanced to see what their friends had received.

The director then asked three of the little boys to show us their sleeping quarters. The 40 x 20 foot sleeping area was crowded but neatly kept. The walls were painted light aqua, stained from years of heavy use, giving me the opinion that the caregivers operated on a very limited budget. Portions of the plaster had fallen, revealing fragile adobe and lathe. The dampness made the room feel much cooler than the outside temperature. The concrete floor had a few rugs spread here and there, but the nap had long since been worn down, leaving only the burlap weave. The forty wrought iron beds were crowded into two rows that ran the length of the room with no space to walk between the beds. The kids climbed in from the foot of the bed. Despite this simplicity, my mind drifted to an orphanage in Liberia where four kids often shared a double bed. At least here each child had a bed to himself. I saw no sheets or blankets, and only two pillows in the whole dorm. Each bed had a burlap mattress that wasn't over a quarter inch thick. It was obviously an effort to keep the children from sleeping directly on the supportive wire mesh. Each child had one wooden box approximately 2 x 3 x 2 ft. Each boy's box was padlocked. The boys explained that their boxes contained all of their earthly possessions—clothes, toys, and books. I asked one boy, "Out of everything in your chest, what is most important to you?" He replied, "My books. I love my books." Then he ran to open his chest to show his limited treasures. In his case, his box was nearly full of books. I nearly cried when I saw another little guy's favorite toy—an axle and its remaining rubber wheels. The body of a car or truck had long since disappeared.

None of the children wore shoes. Most of them had never owned a pair of shoes in their life—their feet were heavily calloused. Given the glass and nails so prevalent on all the community streets, the bottoms of their feet resembled thick leather. They allowed us a peek into the kitchen, but the darkness was as empty as the shelves. Everything was prepared over gas-heating elements. I assumed the groceries were brought in on a daily basis or the children would be hungry for that particular day. I was so overwhelmed by the experience that I moved to the less depressing patio to try to find a few moments alone. Our guides indicated it was time to go, so we waved goodbye to the kids and returned to the busy streets. My mind drifted to Kipling and his poem "Mandalay."

"By the old Moulmein Pagoda, lookin' lazy at the sea,

There's a Burma girl a-settin', and I know she thinks o' me;

For the wind is in the palm-trees, and the Temple-bells they say:

"Come you back, you British soldier; come you back to Mandalay!"

Come you back to Mandalay,...

Can't you 'ear their paddles chunkin' from Rangoon to Mandalay?

On the road to Mandalay ...

Ship me somewhere's east of Suez, where the best is like the worst,

Where there aren't no Ten Commandments an' a man can raise a thirst;

For the Temple-bells are callin', an' it's there that I would be —

By the old Moulmein Pagoda, looking lazy at the sea;

On the road to Mandalay,..."[6]

Dominican Republic 2005

"The Least People of the World"

"The King will reply, 'I tell you the truth, whatever you did for one of the least of these brothers of mine, you did for me.' Then he will say to those on his left, 'Depart from me, you who are cursed, into the eternal fire prepared for the devil and his angels. For I was hungry and you gave me nothing to eat, I was thirsty and you gave me nothing to drink, I was a stranger and you did not invite me in, I needed clothes and you did not clothe me, I was sick and in prison and you did not look after me.' They also will answer, 'Lord, when did we see you hungry or thirsty or a stranger or needing clothes or sick or in prison, and did not help you?' He will reply, 'I tell you the truth, whatever you did not do for one of the least of these, you did not do for me.' Then they will go away to eternal punishment, but the righteous to eternal life" (Matthew 25:40-46).

Overlooking the Caribbean Sea, on the edge of the city of Santo Domingo in the Dominican Republic, stands a monument erected to Christopher Columbus. The government built a mammoth pyramid to honor him. The new structure is called "The Lighthouse." A light in the shape of a cross shines from the top, day and night. You can see crosses inlaid on its outside walls. It looks like a modernistic Christian monument.

Inside, there is a metal box reputed to contain some of the remains of Christopher Columbus. (One has to wonder where the rest of him was deposited.) On the other side of the new highway running in front of the lighthouse is a tall wall that entirely blocks out what stands beyond it. The local people call it the "Wall of Shame."

What we cannot see on the other side of the six foot high wall is a vast neighborhood of shacks. Here, people live in great, indescribable poverty. Thousands of people barely exist with limited drinking water, no proper sewage, sub-standard housing, a pathetic amount of food, and inadequate health care and education.

We cannot literally go behind that wall, but I think you can imagine. Instead I want to take you behind the wall that stands outside our own churches. A wall we have erected in our hearts and minds to dull our sensitivity and to avoid the tug it can place on our lives and lifestyle. We don't desire such exposure.

People of faith need to go there. Why? God cares about the people who live on the other side of the tracks from you. God's heart is always turned toward the poor. And, God implores us to give considerable attention to these people who are really a part of our larger human family. Jesus calls them the LEAST people!

Jesus identified six kinds of least people whom we need to see:

The hungry

The thirsty

The stranger

The naked

The sick

The one in prison

If Jesus were writing a list today, he might include the starving, disenfranchised females, the "unreached" people groups, the abused, the homeless, and people with HIV.

Missions mean doing something today for the "least of these."

U.S.A. 2005

"Recognizing God's Involvement in Your Life"

A spiritual surprise cannot be surpassed. I was visiting the Grace

Community Church in San Francisco, and a longtime friend had been designated to pick me up at the airport to take me to my hotel. After a hello and a hug, we put my suitcase in the backseat of her Nissan and departed for my hotel.

Her first comment came in the form of a question—"How have you seen God working in your life in the last week?" I was speechless. No one had ever asked me such a question. At first, I struggled for a spontaneous reply. I had nothing. Then, I thought, "That is an inappropriate and personal question." The next moment I felt embarrassed because I had not reflected about a question so relevant for a Christian. It seemed like minutes as she waited. My mind replayed many of the events of the last week and I realized that I had not been attentive to God's desire to lead my life. My spiritual life was stagnated and I had not even been concerned.

So, I ask you—"How have you seen God working in your life in the last week?"

Missions involve a vibrant testimony, and your testimony is set on fire through the recognition of God's action in your life. The stories I write are my effort to give ammunition for my testimony when I have the opportunity to use it. I encourage you to write your experiences with God so you will not forget them and so they can enhance your witness.

Mongolia 2006

"Giving Away What You Would Like to Keep!"

Amazing people come in different packages with different virtues. Generous people deserve more recognition then they receive. Giving to someone else what a person would really like to keep is commendable and rare.

Four of us boarded a recycled military van and began the drive from Ulaanbaatar to Zunhera, Mongolia. It would be a 100-mile trip through the high desert. The dilapidated vehicle had long since lost its carpet so our feet rested directly upon metal. We could hear and feel the sand, rocks, and gravel carom off the underside of the van. Already the rust had eroded the floorboard, allowing near freezing air to seep into the van. Thermal underwear and blankets were in the car if the heater failed or we got stranded on the roadside. Our hosts had even packed a few sandwiches, some fresh fruit, and soft drinks for our trip.

Our thin chauffeur made this trip monthly, which was fortunate because the roads appeared to me as almost indistinguishable from the barren desert floor. I knew from experience that these drivers were also miracle mechanics, capable of repairing most breakdowns with wire, string, or rubber bands. The sandy road was free from traffic. Occasionally, we passed a cowboy or two on horseback and they waved wildly in recognition of other signs of life.

Periodically, we saw herds of fat hairy camels. I wondered how they stayed so healthy when nothing green was available to eat. We stopped to observe a small sheep farm lodged into the opening of a mountain canyon. My imagination drifted into the past with visions of Genghis Khan with his spindly beard and his nomad army crossing these plains, slaughtering any civilian resistance unwilling to surrender their animals.

These nomads had one or two *gers* (yurts). These tent-like dwellings were built on wood frames and covered with wool felt. Coal smoke belched from the center of the roof. Two of the farmers chatted near their *ger*. Sheep wandered freely within site of a *gers* and the fold where they were kept safely at night. But the rest of time they appeared to be free to roam.

A mound of blue appeared immediately ahead of us. It looked like a roadblock. The closer we got, the more I focused on what resembled a roadside dump topped by blue flags. It was so striking; I asked the driver to stop and questioned what this memorial heap meant out in the middle of nowhere. He said, "That is an *Ovoo*. They are all over the roadsides. It is the equivalent of a shamanist shrine. Many travelers walk around it three times and place a rock, a coin, or a bone on it. This action entitles them to a 'wind horse,' bringing them good luck on their trek." I stared at the pile of castaways and wondered about the significance of each offering. There were crutches and alcohol bottles. Were these prayers of faith, recognizing or pleading for healing? I left with more questions than answers, hesitant to pursue the discussion.

Our goal was to arrive at the Junhera church for a scheduled 6 p.m. worship service. And, without the congregation's knowledge, we were carrying a surprise that they could never had expected. They would be very curious when we carried the two huge cardboard boxes into the sanctuary. I knew the contents but had yet to see them.

We arrived slightly early. The church was easily identifiable by the four-foot cross at the peak of the roof. A few aged cars were parked haphazardly outside the church. The congregants were watching for us and surrounded our car before we could exit. It was a crowd heavily represented by children and youth. The kids had rosy chubby cheeks, apparently chapped by winds that never rest in Northern Mongolia. One child took my hand and ushered me into the building and out of the chill. The inside of the church was only slightly warmer than outside. The one coal stove was not in use. Everyone wore heavy coats as if preparing to go sledding. Most had stocking caps, neck scarves, or baseball caps, and everyone wore gloves or thrust their hands deep into their pockets.

The pastor was a young man, a bit uncomfortable with his leadership role. He quickly handed over the service to the song leader who urged volunteers to come forward to help with the praise period. Finally, he coerced six people to join his choir. Even though I couldn't understand any of the words, I recognized the tune of "Our God is an Awesome God," and felt the ever-present Spirit of God.

The pastor then assumed the leadership to introduce the guests. The two huge boxes were resting on the right side of the stage. My guide, Ernest Gillis, a missionary to South Korea from the United States, took the pulpit and spoke briefly. Then, he said, "I have a surprise for your church from my church." Smiles moved across the room as if Santa Claus had entered.

Rev. Gillis called the six choir members forward and began to pull from the box blue and white choir robes for each of them. He asked if there were others interested in joining the choir. Before we could count, the choir had grown to fifteen—the number of robes available. The concert that followed was greatly improved by the smiles of all the participants.

I learned the donating church did not yet own choir robes. People actually gave away what they would liked to keep.

Mongolia 2006

"Where Two or Three Gather"

Ulaanbaatar is the capital of Mongolia and has over one million people. It features short warm summers and long bitterly cold and dry winters. It's known as the coldest capital in the world. It was founded as a nomadic Buddhist *ger* (yurt) monastic center, moving from site to site from 1639 until 1778 when it stabilized at its current location.

No capital city in the world struggles with a housing problem like Ulaanbaatar. Sixty percent of its citizens live in *gers* or humble shacks without water, sanitation or basic infrastructure. Heating and cooking is provided with wood or coal burning stoves that create constant pollution, particularly in the winter.

I visited a small new church development that was being sponsored by another newly organized congregation in South Korea. That seemed like a massive project for a small church that had not yet secured property for its own congregation. But, I gradually understood the logic as we drove from the downtown of the capital through neighborhoods of *gers* and wooden shanties. As we started up a winding road toward the top of one of the highest hills in the city, more and more *gers* lined the side of dirt and gravel roads only passable with four-wheel drive jeeps. I was informed we were driving higher and higher on what had been the garbage dump for the city until people in deepest poverty began to invade the area once a new dump had been established on the outskirts of Ulaanbaatar.

A church was built at the peak of the reclaimed dump; and, the appropriate building for the location was a *ger* that would hold approximately thirty people. This house of God was beautifully simple, and brought to mind the scripture—"Where two or three gather in my name, there am I with them" (Matthew 18:20).

South Korea and Afghanistan 2008

"How Will God Work Out This Tragedy?"

Can you imagine a scenario where you could dedicate much of six weeks to prayer and Bible Study? That would be the ultimate, right? Wrong! Every life experience carries the potential for growth, stagnation or retreat. So much of the value of a personal experience depends on perspective and interpretation. What one person considers a positive experience might devastate another. So much depends on an unbending faith that God can be trusted to make every life experience, whether good or bad, serve for our ultimate good and God's glory.

At the prompting of my South Korean host pastor, I visited the Saemmul Church in Seoul on February 1, 2008. It was a large congregation in an upscale southern suburb of Seoul. Twenty-three of this church's members had been kidnapped in Afghanistan in mid-July, 2007. They were held for six weeks while the world watched in fear that every member of the team would be killed. The South Korean government was forced to negotiate the release of the hostages. Many South Koreans assumed that a huge ransom was paid. Those same people resented the imprudence of the church because it had been warned by the South Korean government about the danger of sending missionaries to Afghanistan.

As we started our visit, I asked the minister if I might be able to speak directly with one of those kidnapped. He said, "Actually, one is here." He acted surprised that I would want to speak to him.

In a few minutes, a lean smiling man entered the room. He looked different than the pictures I had seen immediately following their release. I tried to be sensitive with my questions, since I knew that the Taliban had murdered two of their group during their six week captivity.

It turned out that I didn't have to ask but a couple broad questions and he quietly shared his reflections. He interpreted the whole incident as the will of God. His voice only broke one time as he talked about the death of his two friends.

The Afghanis kidnapped the group from their van when it was stopped at a roadblock. Another similar missionary group had been allowed to pass the captors immediately ahead of them, and another bus of workers following them passed undisturbed. A well-intentioned mission trip turned to tragedy in a matter of moments.

In the beginning the missionaries were held together in one group. The Taliban at the time had no idea they were missionaries, only foreigners. The missionaries were dressed in typical Afghan clothing and the men had allowed their beards to grow during their mission trip. The missionaries made some corporate decisions the first night in captivity. First, they would not deny their faith under any circumstance, but would make other compromises as needed in order to preserve their lives. Second, they would state clearly to the Taliban that under no conditions would they attempt to injure or kill any of the kidnappers even if the kidnappers chose to kill them for one reason or another. Third, they would not try to escape.

The media reported that the group was deeply troubled and filled with fear. The man we interviewed said that was actually not the case. Their trust in their pastoral leadership gave them comfort. Upon being kidnapped their guide and mission pastor told them, "Look, I do not think that they will kill us. They have little to gain from such a choice. However, I am convinced that if they do kill someone as an example of their seriousness to secure the requested release of Taliban prisoners, they will only kill one of us. And, I am willing to be that person." This brought constant peace to the remaining members. As it turned out, the pastor was the first to be martyred. Later, another man was also murdered. But, then as the pastor had assumed, there was no more killing.

During captivity, the group was divided into smaller groups of 11 and 12; and, finally into groups of 3, 4 and 6. They assumed this was an effort to avoid a rescue of the entire group. They were often moved at night from one location to another. The missionary we interviewed said the missionaries felt a deep sense of peace. He described it as dwelling in the eye of a hurricane. While their home church and the missionary community were in a high state of concern, God allowed them to feel under God's care. They tried to eat the food, but found most of it terribly different than their normally spicy food. Some of those kidnapped lost more than 20 pounds during the experience.

One of the miracles that occurred during the captivity was that at least one Bible was not confiscated from one member of each group. So, some groups took turns of two hours reading the Bible, passing it from one to another. One other group of four divided their Bible into four parts and then rotated the sections periodically. It was amazing the captors allowed the Bible to remain in the prisoner's possession.

The impact of the kidnapping, the death of two of their group, the uncertainty of six weeks in captivity, and the shunning by many upon their return is not measurable. They find meaning for the loss of life of their two friends by seeing the larger picture of God's will for evangelizing the world. They believe it is one more way God's glory and the love of Christians was made manifest in the midst of unbelievers.

The missionaries' service didn't materialize at all as they planned. The story of the Saemmul missionaries in Afghanistan is still being written. No one fully knows how God will transform such a tragic story to good for those willing to do what they believed to be right.

Central Asia 2009

"Door #1, Door #2, or Door #3"

Since 1963 television contestants have chosen the prizes behind one of three doors on "Let's Make a Deal." The doors usually contain one valuable prize like a car, a smaller prize such as a room of furniture, and a "zonk." The excitement of making a choice with the hope that something valuable rests behind the door of choice thrills audiences and contestants day after day. But, another choice carries a more profound outcome.

Nuria was a timid woman in a house church in one of the *stans* formed after the fall of the Soviet Union. She confessed to being afraid to tell her close friend about her love for Christ, but during a family conference she discovered a new boldness through the stories of other women sharing their faith. So the day after the conference she went to her village, found her friend, and told her the good news. Strangely enough, the two women shared the given name, Nuria.

At first her friend showed little interest. She seemed skeptical saying, "Earlier you believed in Mohammad, now Jesus. It doesn't really make any difference what you believe." Nuria told her, "You think there are many ways to God, but there is only one way. It's the way God provided through Christ." Her friend suddenly realized that what Nuria had told her was the key to explaining her recurring dreams. For the previous two months she kept having the same dream again and again. In her dream there were many doors and she was holding many keys. She kept trying to open the doors, but none of the keys would work and none of the doors would open.

Door #1, Door #2, or Door #3? Nuria's decision determined more than a prize; it included the possibility of a personal relationship with the Son of God and the hope of eternal joy. "Here I am! I stand at the door and knock. If anyone hears my voice and opens the door, I will come in and eat with him, and he with me" (Revelation 3:20).[7]

U.S.A. 2009

"It's Amazing Who Celebrates Christmas"

"...'How awesome are your deeds! So great is your power that your enemies cringe before you. All the earth bows down to you; they sing praise to you, they sing praise to your name'" (Psalm 56:3-4).

I attended the Christmas concert on December 5, 2009, at Coe College in Cedar Rapids, Iowa. A 60-person choir and the excellent Cedar Rapids Symphony entertained us with an inspired performance. As I listened to Bach, Handel, and others, I assumed that none of the composers could have imagined that for centuries God would be praised by people who under no other situation would willingly celebrate the majesty of Jesus. There I sat attentively with 600 people (atheists, Muslims, Jews, Buddhists, animists, and Christians) as God's name was praised through music.

I delighted for the Christian musicians who were able to witness to their love for Christ through their work. They were so fortunate to be able to tell the story of Jesus without offending anyone.

I also thought of the academy award winning film—*Chariots of Fire*. It is the story of two British athletes, one a devout Christian missionary, Eric Liddell, and a determined Jew, Harold Abrahams, who competed in the 1924 Olympics.

Eric Liddell states in the film, "You came to see a race today, to see someone win. It happened to be me. But I want you to do more than just watch a race. I want you to take part in it. I want to compare faith to running in a race. It's hard. It requires concentration of will, energy of soul." He goes on to admit that he has no secret formula to win a race and that everyone has to run in his or her own way. He argues that the power to see a race comes from within the person running the race. He paraphrases Jesus, "Behold, the Kingdom of God is within you. If with all your hearts, you truly seek me, you shall surely find me." He insists that if people will commit themselves to the love of Christ, then, that is how to run a straight race.

Everything Liddell did was to point to the glory of God, which is what our lives should be about, my friends. Our lives should point to the reality that God is so great that all peoples should fall to their knees and praise him. "Say to God, 'How awesome are your deeds! So great is your power that your enemies cringe before you. All the earth bows down to you; they sing praise to you, they sing praise to your name'" (Psalm 66:3-4).

Israel 2012

"A Quiet Dove"

This walk was memorable. I wish you could have joined us. For most of those privileged to make this pilgrimage, it was a once in a lifetime experience. Seldom can you hop off a bus and be standing at the edge of the Jordan River—the river where John baptized Jesus.

The Israeli government promotes two sites for pilgrims to use for baptisms and other affirmations of faith. The Office of Tourism opened the Yardenit site in 1981 to replace the original site of Kasser Al Yahud at the southern end of the Jordan, near the city of Jericho and within sight of the Dead Sea. Even though the Yahud site is probably the most likely site for the baptism of Jesus, Yardenit remains the most popular.

As we walked the sidewalk to the entry into the dressing rooms, restaurant, shops, and steps down to the river, we saw Mark 1:9-11 written on mosaic tiles in multiple languages. We paused in front of the English mural and read: "At that time Jesus came from Nazareth in Galilee and was baptized by John in the Jordan. Just as Jesus was coming up out of the water, he saw heaven being torn open and the Spirit descending on him like a dove. And a voice came from heaven: 'You are my Son, whom I love; with you I am well pleased.'"

It only took a few seconds for us to pass through the entry booth. The Jordan, probably twenty feet below the level where we stood, drew our attention. The view took our breath; the experience was surreal. Shades of greens, grays, and browns dominated the landscape. Trees and shrubs, such as apple of Sodom, tamarisk, and rhododendron, bordered the river. Only the sky was light blue. A slight breeze cooled the riverside.

We heard pilgrims singing in more than one language. Many of the visitors at the river's edge wore white baptismal robes, waiting for their moment of baptism or reaffirmation. Despite several ceremonies occurring at different baptismal areas side-by-side along the river, we soon focused upon our own service.

The baptisms that took place within our group were definitely a significant moment in the life of the participants. Most of life's moments come and go almost without notice. We hardly pause to distinguish one from the other. Many times we wonder if God chooses to enter directly into the lives of people? Is God mostly an observer? Just how personal is God? Why would the Creator want to relate to the creature? Since God is omnipresent and infinitely loving, what would restrict him from always being by our side? Since the Jordan is such a sacred place, could we expect God's special presence in this place?

Jesus once said, "Anyone who loves me will obey my teaching. My Father will love them, and we will come to them and make our home with them" (John 14:23). The personal nature of God is often confirmed in God's unique, sometimes silent, appearance in daily life.

Some of us headed to dressing rooms to change into our white ankle-length gowns. As we approached the water's edge, the tall plumed river grass waved in the gentle breeze. We fortunately came at the end of the day as more and more pilgrims were finalizing their services and leaving the area.

Another minister and I baptized the others. All four had chosen immersion. This mode of baptism was uncommon for us, so we helped one another. It is still a rather strenuous process and I wondered how 3,000 people could be baptized by immersion in a single day. But then my mind shifted from mode to significance.

We finished the baptisms, and Mark and I stood face-to-face looking into one another's eyes; we decided at that moment to reaffirm our baptism by cupping our hands and pouring water upon one another. It was a special moment, but the experience didn't climax with the falling of the water from our head back to its source. We stood up to our thighs in gently flowing waters as small fish nibbled on our feet and legs. None of us wanted to leave this sacred place or walk away from such a precious moment. As we began to leave the water and climb the underwater steps to the riverbank, quietly a brown dove glided in and quietly landed on a handrail three feet from us. Someone exclaimed, "LOOK AT THAT!" We stood quietly for a moment and then walked the rest of the way to the bank.

I am so glad our whole group was present to share this appearance of a dove on the bank of the Jordan. Granted it didn't land on one of our shoulders and there was no audible voice affirming God's presence. Some will say it was a coincidence. But, I choose to believe that God wanted us to know that the Holy Spirit was there to bless this significant moment in our lives.

Tanzania 2013

"The News We Prefer to Ignore"

For those of us that worship freely, it is good to remember that many people of all faiths face life-threatening persecution. The Voice of the Martyrs has a web site that posts with frequency the violation of freedom of worship around the world. The following was posted about Christians in Tanzania.

"On June 2, Pastor Robert Ngai in Geita, northeastern Tanzania, was attacked by a large group of radical Muslims. The attackers broke into his home and attacked him with machetes. The pastor received serious cuts on his hands and arms when he raised his arms to protect his head from the blows. The injuries were beyond local doctors' ability to treat, so he was rushed to a hospital in a nearby, larger city for treatment. Ngai is the pastor of the Evangelical Assemblies of God Church. At last word from VOM contacts, he was still in ICU. Two nights before the attack on Pastor Ngai, the home of Pastor Daudi Nzumbi in Geita also came under attack. Pastor Nzumbi leads the Free Pentecostal Church of Tanzania (FPCT) in Geita. Thankfully, the attackers fled after they were confronted by Pastor Nzumbi's large, barking dogs. When Pastor Nzumbi called the police, the officer in charge told him, 'I cannot protect every pastor!'"

Many people are totally unaware of the frequent religious persecution in the world. Part of the church's responsibility is to inform people about the opposition that many people of faith face daily. We must find effective ways to advocate for the human rights of all people.[8]

U.S.A. 2013

"Opening and Closing Your Heart"

"But whoever has the world's goods, and beholds his brother in need and closes his heart against him, how does the love of God abide in him? Dear children, let us not love with words or speech but with actions and in truth" (1 John 3:17).

The desire to help people in need exists in the heart of the Christian. It is a by-product of the presence of love in the heart of a person touched personally by Christ and through the indwelling of the Holy Spirit. Unfortunately providing help isn't a simple process of writing a check. The following are points to serve as a guide for people who are attempting to decide whether to help a person who appears to need assistance.

1) The evaluation of a real need requires careful analysis. Not every request for assistance justifies an investment of time and money. Even though it is easy to pull a few dollars from one's wallet or purse, this is not always the most helpful response.

2) Before deciding about a need, it is crucial to hear the story behind the request. Everyone, despite our best efforts, may reject a real need because of a bias or prejudice. Perhaps, the need comes from a Moslem, a person with HIV, a member of the KKK, a Mormon, a prostitute, a gypsy, a person with body odor, a Christian, and the list continues; a real need remains a need regardless of the person bearing its burden. It takes time to get past appearance and profiling to see the heart, body and soul of the person in need.

3) Many requests are repetitive and need a long-term response to avoid an endless dependency on assistance from one person or another. For example, a single mother may feel driven to prostitution because she lacks the education or training to earn a livable income. Such a problem requires a plan to support the family while the mother is receiving training.

4) Some needs demand immediate help. In such cases, there is no time to investigate or run the issue by a committee. The caregiver/donor must generously meet the need while being certain the recipient spends the money honestly.

5) Valid financial help seldom exceeds a Christian and his or her church's ability to meet the need in one-way or another. In other words, people should not be denied without careful thought and prayer.

6) Some people do not merit help. Some people can care for themselves, but are simply prone to ask others to do their work for them. "No" is sometimes a valid response to requests for aid.

7) Apart from minor gifts for gas and food, responsible giving requires follow-up. Lending a helping hand often involves the witness of love. This love can only be achieved when the donor forms a caring relationship with the person in need. Such care often requires hours of concern and assistance.

8) It is better to error by providing help to a person who actually has no need than to turn away a person with a real need.

"And do not neglect doing good and sharing; for with such sacrifices God is pleased" (Hebrews 13:16).

People wishing to get involved in the "Mighty Acts of God" must move their ministry of service to the front lines where needs are most prominent. This often means leaving our homes, pews, and even our country. The willingness to say, "I am available" is the beginning of serving in partnership with God. And, that is really where spirituality is found and edified.

SECTION 2

Spiritual Stories as a Form of Witness

Hints about Writing and Telling the Story

It is my hope people hearing or reading my stories will be motivated to write and tell their stories. Section two provides some of the basics of story writing. Everyone is a storyteller. Some are just better than others. Think about how many times you say or hear, "I remember," "You should have been there," or "Now listen to this." Those are phrases that indicate the speaker is about to weave a tale of one sort or another.

I used to play a game with my grandchildren in order to tell my stories. I called it "Truth or Fiction." I would weave a tale and then ask them to guess if it was true or fictitious. This game excited their interest while allowing me to testify to many of the "mighty acts" of God in my life or expose them to some of our family lore. I hoped some of the stories would be etched in their minds and that some of the children would take up the family tradition of storytelling.

As mentioned earlier, our life is a series of moments. They follow one after another in endless succession. A series of moments make an experience. It is fair to say that most moments are hardly discernable and seldom processed. Brief experiences only provide a small effect on our life and are then filed in our subconscious and eventually forgotten. However, important transformational experiences impact our life in one way or another in terms of who we are as a person. As Sue Monk Kidd wrote in the *Secret Life of Bees*, "Stories have to be told or they die, and when they die, we can't remember who we are or why we're here."[8] The sum of our experiences determines who we are. Hence, it is important to write to understand our personal identity and our purpose.

But there is one more important reason to recognize and write stories. Our stories are one of the best ways we have to witness without presumption to the "mighty acts of God." Jesus commissioned his disciples to be his witnesses. "But you will receive power when the Holy Spirit comes on you; and you will be my witnesses in Jerusalem, and in all Judea and Samaria, and to the ends of the earth" (Acts 1:8). He was really asking them to be His story writers and tellers. Accordingly, that responsibility has now been handed on to us. Through the careful writing and telling of our stories, we shift a story about "me," and use it as a testimony that demonstrates God's intimate role in the life of people. Our stories are probably the best way we have to share our faith. Stories remind the listener that God is actively pursuing every human on earth. His pursuit is universal and transcends religion, nationality, and race. That pursuit is a moment-by-moment process with significant events occurring at unforeseen and unpredictable times. The most spiritual people of the world may arguably be those who carefully build a structure in their life that heightens their awareness of God's interaction in their life.

Some of the best of life is lost because important experiences are not recognized, are not written, and are not retold. If you don't think your story is important enough to write and tell, then you have missed so much of what God has been trying to share with you. Your story is a *love story* about God's love for you.

Many people question the strength of a story. A Jewish story of two lovely ladies answers the question quite poignantly.

"Once upon a time, there were two exceedingly beautiful women who lived together in small house at the end of a village. Their names were Truth and Story. One day, the two women were having a discussion that turned into an argument. They debated which of the two of them was the most beautiful and which one was most accepted by the neighbors.

When the argument failed to reach a compromise, they decided to settle it by having a contest. The contest required each woman, one at a time, to walk through the village and see which one could attract the largest following.

Truth was the first to walk down the village street. The villagers tending their gardens and chatting to each other along the road noticed Truth walking towards them. Slowly, they eased back into their houses until there were only a few people tending their gardens. By the time Truth reached the end of the road, she had no one with whom to talk.

She wondered, "What can I do to make myself even more attractive?" She decided there was only one solution left to her, so she removed her robe and stood in the road completely naked. She walked back to her house thinking that the people would surely flock to her now. But in actual fact, the opposite occurred. What few people were left outside fled back to their house and closed their shutters. Truth walked that whole path back to her house completely alone.

When Truth entered her house, her sister greeted her. Story grasped her hands and asked "So? How did it go?"

"I can't believe it," cried Truth. "I walked most of road alone!

Everyone hid themselves from me!" So Story said, "Let me try." She put on her finest robes and jewelry and left the house, walking down to the village. As she walked down the village street, the doors and the shutters flew open and the people came out in droves, smiling and chatting with each other happily. Story walked down the village street and the people followed her, hanging on her every word. When Story turned and walked back through the village, all the people gathered together in the center of the village and celebrated her visit.

She returned to her house and found Truth sitting there, quite humbled. "You win," she said. "It's obvious to me now that Story is more powerful than Truth." But Story took Truth's hand and said, "It's not that Story is more powerful. It's just that nobody likes the Truth, and especially when it is the Naked Truth. If you want to get your point across to your listeners, what you need is the mantle of Story." So she removed her robes and her jewelry, adorned Truth with them, and sent her out into the village. This time, the people opened their doors and windows and flocked towards Truth because now they were open to what she had to say.[9]

You can learn to write and tell stories. The process is relatively simple. But it does require concentration, effort and time. Five steps will put you on the path to developing a story in a written form that can be shared for generations.

First, you must identify an event worthy of sharing. Story writers and tellers constantly monitor their memories and lives for an experience that merits retelling. I personally like to maintain a journal that records the most important experiences of my life. These entries, whether written in detail or only preserved in the form of notes, provide the germinal content for the writing of my stories.

People often ask me, "Where do you get your stories?" For

inspirational stories I look to experiences that move me emotionally. I have to feel a spiritual moment in order to communicate those feelings to another person. Some of my best spiritual or inspirational stories come from what I would call "goose-bump" moments. Those moments often occur when I sense the Holy Spirit is trying to teach me something important. When that happens, I always look for a possible story that begs to be written.

Sometimes reflection about an experience will confirm or illustrate a particular passage of scripture. The pairing of an experience with an appropriate scripture often makes for a good story. You have already read such a story earlier in the chronological stories of this book. It is titled "Emmaus Road Experience" (p. 44).

Usually I prefer to use my own experiences for inspiration. I am certain of the integrity of those stories and feel comfortable with their content. With emotionally laden stories, remember listeners can only appreciate the crescendo for a limited amount of time. If I observe a transitional moment when someone's life is changed forever, I like to shape the remainder of a story around it. That impact moment becomes my focal point.

But, stories also come from non-personal sources. Often, I read or hear an exceptional story that someone else wrote or told. Telling someone else's story is certainly acceptable, if proper credit is given. In fact, most storytellers borrow their material from others. Who has not told biblical stories such as The Good Samaritan, The Prodigal Son, or The Loaves and Fishes? And, almost all parents have oft repeated nursery rhymes, tall tales, or ghost stories.

I look for stories that have a plot—with a need and an answer. People easily identify with a tale about a villain and a hero. Listeners warm easily to themes and stories that many people have imagined or experienced—like snakes, drowning, illness, costly mistakes, sadness, embarrassing moments, fishing, marriage, pets, siblings, vacations, etc.

Second, once you have an idea, you must take the time necessary to write the story. The keys to inspirational or entertaining stories are organization and creative writing. Very few people have the ability to spin an extemporaneous story from a memory. Instead, the best stories emerge from recollection, research, structuring, and writing. When I sit down to write, I elaborate an outline with as many ideas as I can muster on the theme. Writing a story mimics squeezing the water out of a towel. One good wrenching is not enough. You usually need to squeeze it three or four times to get out all the water that your strength will allow. And, then if you let the towel set for a time, and squeeze it again—a little more water will fall into the sink. Good writing takes similar effort. For me, the preparation of my ideas for a particular story varies depending on whether the story is an effort to communicate truth or to entertain. When I am retelling a story about God's interaction in my life or in the life of another, I am compelled to rely on the impact of the actual event to empower the story. I do not have the editorial privilege to interject material into such a story to make it more exciting or amazing than it actually was.

However, when I am writing a story to entertain, I do have the freedom to expand the material and incidentals to add to the impact of the story. I can make the story occur wherever I choose. I can create unique, even conflictive characters. I can amend conversations to make them funnier. My creativity is free to roam. There is a line in the movie, *The Magic of Belle Isle*, where Morgan Freeman gives a neighbor girl advice related to writing. He tells the young girl, "Imagination is the most powerful force ever made available to humankind…it is seeing what's not there."

When writing to entertain, your imagination is your best friend. My best stories begin with a few exciting kernels from my memory or a journal. I let myself, or force myself, to enter into the experience looking both backward and forward from the kernels, and write where my imagination leads me. This involves seeing the people who were or could have been involved, the details of the physical setting, the humor or seriousness of the moment, the conversations that could or did occur, etc., always seeking an instinctive conclusion.

Writers and tellers of stories find ways to connect their story with the audience. Questions enable this to happen. For example, if talking about the spiritual gift of hospitality, you might ask, "How many of you know a person who always makes you feel welcome his or her home?" Or, if you are telling a snake story, "Do snakes give you the heebie-jeebies? Questions usually compel the audience to respond to a story either verbally or non-verbally, thus keeping them involved.

If you are telling a personal story, don't be afraid to express your vulnerability or weakness. Doing so immediately helps the audience to see your humanity and identify you as a possible friend. It is important to reveal emotions like fear, joy, pain, sadness, and laughter. Your story becomes more believable with the expression of such emotions. In contrast, an audience can easily see through a teller who attempts to express an emotion that is not real.

Third, I believe it is important that you memorize your story if you intend to tell it. There is a difference between reading poetry and telling a story. Poetry demands word-by-word reading. Its rhyme and meter can be lost if words are omitted or changed. The telling of a story begs for the freedom to drift from the written text. A written story allows the writer to explore and organize thoughts carefully, but the script is not sacred and the teller does not have to follow it word-for-word. The idea is to repeat the story over and over until the teller is comfortable enough to "freewheel" a memorized story. Storytellers often alter and enhance their stories through spontaneous comments and non-verbal reactions from the audience. When you find spontaneous lines in a presentation that are particularly effective, incorporate them into the written script as soon as possible and make them a part of the story so you do not omit them in future opportunities to tell the story.

Fourth, you should practice your story. I like to tell my stories while standing. It sets free the actor in me to appear when needed. It allows me the freedom to approach or distance myself from the audience. I like to do my practice in a private place. I might use my study or go out to a park when no one is present. It is helpful to practice a story five to ten times before telling it to an audience. Sometimes it is beneficial to video your practice so you can see yourself the way the audience sees you. This practice often reveals dead spots, annoying gestures, poor eye contact or other factors that diminish the effectiveness of your presentation.

Fifth, you must eventually face a live audience. Every storyteller must identify places to tell his or her stories. Ask yourself *What audience is appropriate for my stories?* Or, *Is this particular story appropriate for a particular audience?* This decision is crucial for successful storytelling. Begin by identifying people or groups from among your immediate list of contacts who will give you the opportunity to speak. Some examples include: Civic Clubs, Storytelling Groups, Retreats, Worship Services, Conventions, Christian Schools, Bible Colleges, Mission Conferences, Continuing Education Events, Local Churches, and Retirement Resorts.

For a novice, the first few events are intimidating, fear-filled, and nearly crippling. But, each opportunity to present raises the comfort level of the teller. Your audience is really your best friend. Almost all audiences tend to provide the best response to the novice that could be expected. Many times storytelling is like karaoke, everyone gets applause. Eventually, you will cease to think so much about your methodology and the content of the story, and begin to interact with and adjust to the audience. If you are truly confident in the content of your story, you can then reveal your interest in your audience. The word "you" shouldn't be underestimated. It is a certain magnet to pull in your audience. Many speakers use the word "us" or "me" too often. "Talking with" is much more effective than "speaking to" an audience. The tone of speaking sets the mood for the presentation. A parental tone sends a message of superiority and control. A conversational tone communicates friendship and congeniality. Of course, if you are developing a particular character in the story who is angry and obnoxious, then the tone and volume depends on the persona you want to telegraph to the mind of the listener.

Good storytellers are experts in matching their stories to the majority of the people in the audience. A series of three inspirational stories, good as they may be, will probably not be well received at a secular based men's club. Three wildly funny stories with subtle innuendos will likely get a cool reception in a church setting.

It is helpful to ask yourself as a storyteller, *What is the purpose of this story?* For example, does the story intend to inspire? Or, is the story an attempt to help people evaluate the importance of forgiveness and reconciliation? Storytellers need to know the purpose of a particular story in order to evaluate if they have communicated the story well enough for the audience to understand the purpose.

An inspirational story should be allowed to develop its own impact. The Holy Spirit is going to work under, above and within the story. In fact, the Holy Spirit may be speaking to a listener about something entirely different than the story being told. As with the parables of

Jesus, the storyteller does not always have to interpret the meaning of a particular story. Instead, it may be better to rely on the Holy Spirit to make a lasting impression on the mind or heart of the listener if it is needed. As I retrace my life searching for transformational moments, they have usually happened when the Spirit spoke in that mysterious small voice and not because someone tried to force or manipulate a response.

However, people are passive by nature and need to be reminded that Christianity and all forms of spirituality are action oriented. *Go* and *Do* are very important two letter words in Christianity. Much of Christian history is written about people who went and did, while not much is written about people who chose a passive route. Consequently, inspirational stories are told to motivate, to convict, to encourage, and to teach. Again, the Holy Spirit, not the storyteller, will ultimately be the interpreter of a story. Any long-term results from listening to an inspirational storyteller will result because God chooses to shape a person's life and that person responds in willing obedience.

The scripture is clear about the importance of storytelling. "But how can they call on him to save them unless they believe in him? And how can they believe in him if they have never heard about him? And how can they hear about him unless someone tells them?" (Romans 10:14). The use of stories to communicate your personal experiences with God is arguably the best tool you have at your disposal to encourage spiritual reflection. It is crucial to realize the incredible importance and power of a story. One of your stories may be the tool that God will use to call an individual into a deeper relationship with him. What an opportunity and a responsibility!

So, write and tell a story, it will enrich your life and the lives of others. It is one of best ways to communicate your faith.

NOTES

[1] Erin Morgenstern, *The Night Circus*, Random House, New York, 2011.

[2] Written by James M. Weber, missionary to Japan. Original version appeared in *Let's Quit Kidding Ourselves About Missions*, Moody Press, 1979 by The Moody Bible Institute. Edited and revised by Howard Culbertson.

[3] The lyrics for "Blood-Stained Glory" are copied from Wikipedia, the free encyclopedia under the Creative Commons AttributionShare-Alike License.

[4] Adapted from a testimony written by Michele Gentry de Correal, Armenia, Colombia.

[5] Rudyard Kipling, "Mandalay," 1919. The selected portions of "Mandalay" are copied from www.PoemHunter.com under the Creative Commons Attribution Share-Alike License.

[6] The personal names and the geographical location in this story have been changed for the purpose of confidentiality.

[7] This story is used with permission from a web post by the Voice of the Martyrs at www.persecution.com.

[8] Sue Monk Kidd, *The Secret Life of Bees*, Penguin Books, New York, NY, 2002.

[9] A popular Jewish story. Adapted from a podcast by Brian Sturm, Assistant Professor, University of North Carolina at Chapel Hill.

Robert B. Watkins

A Study Guide

Introduction

The following study guide accompanies the individual stories found in *God's Mighty Acts Around the Globe* by Robert Watkins. The primary purpose of the study guide is to elevate mission awareness and involvement. The author suggests each participant read the assigned story prior to the class/study session. However, do not assume that everyone has read the story prior to the group session. The sessions are not dated to allow for more flexibility in terms of time spent on each session. The discussion for some stories might take longer than one session, depending on the interest of the group. The stories, the discussion questions, and the website suggestions can easily provide enough material for a year or longer. It is a matter of interest and time constraints.

Intentionally, the variety of the material should provoke thought and action for all types of church groups. Groups can use the guide as a discipleship resource in a church school setting. Or, it could serve as a small group study for a mission team or church mission committee. Home Bible study groups may want to use it as an approach to study selected scriptures related to missions. It can serve as a devotion guide for a family or as a study for two friends wanting to increase their understanding of and commitment to the different nuances of missions.

A passage of scripture has been selected that links well with the story and/or theme. A mission discussion theme is identified for each story, followed by numerous questions to facilitate significant thought and discussion about each theme. One or more activities are suggested for each story. In as much as possible, the activities relate to the theme of the story, but in a few cases the activities explore a different mission concern. These possibilities are always in the form of web-links that were active at the time of the printing of the study guide. The content of each link comes from a variety of para-church organizations, denominational sources, or individuals who have provided articles or other information for websites. Naturally, it would be ideal for the group to have access to the web during the study sessions, but in many cases the leader will need to bring copies of the important content of the website to the session. These suggestions are included to stimulate ideas for people who are interested in strengthening mission effectiveness and exploring personal spirituality. They are not endorsed in their entirety by any one denomination or the author, but instead they provide exposure to different perspectives on mission thought and action.

The goal of including these links is to save the reader time in seeking thought-provoking material about mission subjects. Many websites could be selected for each activity possibility. So, do not allow the group to get bogged down with theological or practical points with which individuals personally agree or disagree. The idea is to hold up each story, theme, or activity to the authority of the Bible. Years ago, a wise man told his pastor that he often said, "I think," in the body of his sermons. The observer said, "People don't care what you think; they want to know what the Bible says!" The Bible is always the best source upon which to base our belief.

If a suggested website has been discontinued since the publication of the guide, the leader can do a web search for the particular theme/activity being explored and find a site appropriate for the group's interests.

U.S.A. 1993

"A Musical Gift to Remember"   p. ix

Discussion Theme: Using Talents and Spiritual Gifts for Evangelism

1. Locate definitions for *talent* and *spiritual gift*. Write each definition so that the entire group can see them. How do these two classifications differ?

2. Romans 12 mentions the gifts of prophecy, service, teaching, encouragement, giving, administration, and mercy as spiritual gifts.

Which of those gifts do members of your group possess? How are they being used? First Corinthians 11 and Ephesians 4 list other spiritual gifts.

3. Do you believe every Christian is given a spiritual gift? Why? Why not? What is the biblical rationale for your belief? Identify the Bible text most often used to affirm that each Christian is given at least one spiritual gift.

4. Help each member of your study group identify his or her spiritual gift/gifts utilizing an online assessment tool. Discuss why people often fear using their spiritual gifts.

Activity Possibility—Spiritual Gifts Assessment

Two links to a free spiritual gifts assessment are available below. The study leader may want to utilize one of these tools during the class time or during another time decided upon by the group.

http://www.lifeway.com/Article/Women-Leadership-Spiritual-gifts-growth-service

The United Methodist Church also provides a similar assessment.

http://www.umc.org/site/c.lwL4KnN1LtH/b.8051415/

"God's Mighty Acts Around the Globe"   p. 1

Discussion Theme: Calling and Motivation

1. When is the first time you remember God speaking personally to you? Allow 15 minutes for the telling of these stories.

2. How might telling your life stories bring glory to God? (Exploring these study questions over the next few weeks will help you to do this.)

3. Apart from compassion, what motivates you to serve others? Explain the motivating factors and how they drive you to action.

4. What would you identify as one of the most important transitional

moments in your life? Why? Give time for group members to share a life-transforming experience.

5. With what part of Paul's conversion story can you identify personally? Besides hearing about Jesus, what other steps occurred for Paul to respond to God? What elements of Paul's conversion are similar to your own? Do you believe in the importance of a conversion experience? Why or why not?

6. As you recall times when you have felt God's touch in your life, was it due to an outside stimuli or did the experience sort of sneak up on you? How do you distinguish between God's voice and your personal introspection or meditation?

7. Have you sensed a personal call to one type of mission service or another? Allow time for the group to share their stories of call. Explore how different individuals have responded to similar aspects of call (i.e. some may go on work trips, others provide financial backing, and others lend support through prayer).

8. Many people are not called to serve full-time in ministry. To what particular form of service in the church do you feel God is calling you? How have those tugs changed throughout your life?

9. "How beautiful upon the mountains are the feet of him who brings good news, who proclaim peace, who bring good tidings, who proclaim salvation, who say to Zion, 'Your God reigns'" (Isaiah 52:7). What are the implications of this verse for the mission ministry of a local church, particularly your church?

10. What is the role of the church in encouraging peace, happiness, and conversion.

11. Homework: Write for five to ten minutes about a close encounter you have had with God. Then, during the following class session, allow time for participants to share their stories with others.

Activity Possibility—Identifying Your Call

The following links provide ideas for identifying a person's calling or purpose.

http://www.crosswalk.com/faith/spiritual-life/10-ways-to-determine-gods-calling-in-your-life-1326623.html

http://tinybuddha.com/blog/find-your-calling-5-steps-to-identify-your-purpose/

Costa Rica 1975

"Joy to the World, Friends Have Come"   p. 11

Discussion Theme: **Loneliness and Friendship**

1. "This is what the Lord says: Do what is just and right. Rescue from the hand of the oppressor the one who has been robbed. Do no wrong or violence to the foreigner, the fatherless or the widow, and do not shed innocent blood in this place" (Jeremiah 22:3).

2. What life experiences made you feel the most out of your comfort zone? Why were you in those circumstances? How did the experience change your perspective? Did the experience bring you joy or sadness? Did your sadness eventually turn to joy?

3. What experiences have you had trying to learn another language? How do you feel about immigrants who live in your country but cannot speak your language well? What would be the most loving response you or your church could make to such immigrants?

4. What role do holidays play in your life? Which holiday is your favorite? Why?

5. Think about people you know, especially immigrants. How can you or your church extend friendship to these people during holidays?

6. Loneliness cripples even emotionally strong people. Have your study group define loneliness. What age groups are most likely to face loneliness? Does your church have programs to assist people facing loneliness? Invite group participants to identify a specific

person (or group of persons) in your community who is lonely and develop a strategy to help that person feel appreciated and loved.

7. Do you think missionaries are lonely people? Why might missionary kids be lonely? Does your church have anyone responsible for communicating with a specific missionary family?

8. What is the meaning of the incarnation? The term *incarnational love* is usually reserved for the acts of Jesus. When we try to emulate the sacrificial love of Jesus, what should we call such behavior?

9. Second Timothy 4:9-10*a*, 14*a* deals with the importance of visits and encouragement for Paul. "Do your best to come to me quickly, for Demas, because he loved this world, has deserted me and has gone to Thessalonica...Alexander the metalworker did me a great deal of harm..." How do these verses speak to your responsibility for other Christians? Do you feel your church should send one of your members, gifted in encouragement, to visit a missionary?

Activity Possibility—Using a Church Mission Profile

Your church can benefit from using a mission profile to evaluate your current program. Here are two such tools available online. Churches willing to take these assessments and make adjustments will be strengthened.

http://www.cartpioneers.org/content/MissionsAssessmentProfile.pdf

http://www.davidmays.org/Strategy/Strategy%20Leader's%20Guide%20v1.2pdf.pdf

Costa Rica 1975

"Metaphorically Speaking"   p. 13

Discussion Theme: Practicing What You Believe

1. What do you believe to be the key factors for a Christian's witness to make an impact in his or her community? Have the group list its top five factors.

2. Read Ephesian 5:7-14.

3. What three components make up "walking in the light"?

4. Why do you think most behaviors we hide from other people are probably indicators of our points of greatest weakness in living obediently?

5. Do you really believe a Christian has a better life than an unbeliever? Why? What advantages do Christians have?

6. If the Christian lifestyle is significantly better, why do people not ask us about our faith?

7. Today's story speaks of the people who want to be bullfighters and the one's who exit the ring quickly when the action begins. How do you think Christians have conformed to the pressures of culture in the last fifty years? Which of these compromises are the most dangerous for our personal spiritual development? Have we compromised at the point of our basic creed (I believe) or our conduct (I act)? In what ways are you personally concerned enough to struggle against the "watering down" of the Christian faith?

Activity Possibility—Training Mission Leaders

Many churches name people to spearhead their mission program without providing any training. Is that fair? There are many denominational and parachurch conferences in all regions of the globe to train mission leaders. Would your church consider paying the expenses for one or more of your leaders to receive training? Brigada is a wonderful website that posts important mission events across the globe.

www.brigada.org

Urbana is the most widely known mission conference in the world among university students. The site is packed with a plethora of mission resources.

www.urbana.org

Colombia 1976

"The Sharing of a Special Meal"   p. 15

Discussion Theme: **Loneliness, Culture Shock, and Immigrants**

1. What meal would you consider as one of the most significant of your life? Why?

2. Define culture shock. Have you experienced culture shock?

3. If you have experienced culture shock, what actions by others brought you out of the doldrums?

4. Do you know any international people who live in your community? How did you get acquainted with them? Are they relatively new in your community? Have you ever considered that they might be going through culture shock?

5. Are international people part of the ministry of your church? What would your church need to do to prepare for an international outreach in your town or city?

6. "When a foreigner resides among you in your land, do not mistreat them. The foreigner residing among you must be treated as your native-born. Love them as yourself, for you were foreigners in Egypt" (Leviticus 19:33-34). Is there a contemporary significance of this Old Testament passage? What is it? Is your church taking it seriously?

Activity Possibility—Service Evangelism with Internationals

People from countries other than your own are often those most receptive to the good news of Christ. An international ministry may spark new energy in your life or the life of your church.

http://www.namb.net/internationals/

http://www.namb.net/Mobilize_Your_Church_to_LoveLoud/

Colombia 1976

"A Taxi Driver Becomes the Good Samaritan"   p. 18

Discussion Theme: **The Good Samaritan Mentality Versus Stereotyping**

1. The power of influence over other individuals lies within the grasp of each of us. In almost every situation there are a leaders and followers. In this story from Colombia, who were the leaders? Who were the followers?

2. Allow ten minutes for members to write a contemporary story of the Good Samaritan. If you choose not to do so, use the following story.

A Paraphrase of Parable of the Good Samaritan (Luke 10:25-37)

On one occasion a church elder versed in his church's doctrine stood up to test his minister. He asked, "What must I do to inherit eternal life?"

"What does the Bible say?" The minister responded.

The elder answered, "'Love the Lord your God with all your heart and with all your soul and with all your strength and with all your mind and love your neighbor as yourself.'"

"You have answered correctly," the preacher replied. "Do this and you will live."

But the elder wanted to justify himself, so he asked the preacher, "And who is my neighbor?"

In reply the preacher said: "A Christian tourist from Missouri was driving his rental car from Jericho to Jerusalem in Israel when the steering on his car failed and he ran into a concrete wall, flipping the car. His arm was nearly severed, but he remained trapped inside the overturned car. A Christian tour bus happened to be going down the same road. When the people saw the car, they didn't stop because they didn't want to be late for their appointment to see the Garden of Gethsemane. A Jewish resident of Jericho came to the scene of the accident and saw the trapped man, but passed by on the way to a business commitment.

A young Moslem woman was the next to pass in her car, just as the man's car began to burn. Having pity on the man, she quickly swung to the side of the road and jumped out. She ran to the car and forced open the door. The lady tugged the man out and assisted him to her car. He was now bleeding profusely. She sped away to the nearest hospital as the man became unconscious. She checked him into the hospital, using her credit card to guarantee payment for his treatment. She stayed at the emergency room until she was assured he was going to be okay. And, then, she disappeared and returned to her travel.

"Which of these three do you think was a neighbor to the man who had an accident in a foreign land?"

The elder replied, "The lady who had mercy on him."

Jesus told him, "Go and do likewise."

3. Do you find the paraphrase of scripture is helpful in communicating the gospel? Why? Why not? What is your favorite paraphrase of the Bible? What is the difference between a paraphrase and a translation of the Bible?

4. What is your most memorable moment of being befriended by a "Good Samaritan?" How do you define *neighbor*?

5. Why do emergencies tend to bring out the best in people?

6. Research deeply into the story of the "Good Samaritan." Who were the Samaritans? Why did the Jews dislike the Samaritans? Why do you think Jesus placed this situation on the road from Jericho to Jerusalem? Does the road exist today? Do Samaritans exist today? Is there still an antagonism between Samaritans and other Jews?

7. What, if any, similarities are there between many people's dislike of Moslems and the Jew's dislike for the Samaritans? Were your feelings about Muslims changed by the events of September 11th or the "Boston Marathon Bombing?" How? Do you know a Muslim personally? What have you learned about the Muslim faith? Could

you invite a Muslim, a Jew, and a Palestinian to your study group to discuss the above paraphrase of the Good Samaritan? What are the values of inter-faith discussions? How should they be moderated to insure a beneficial experience for all people involved?

8. Do you have any close friends other than Christians? How do your friendships with non-Christians differ from your Christian friendships?

Activity Possibility—Understanding Moslems

Stereotyping is a dangerous practice for Christians who should try to exemplify tolerance and acceptance in their community. How much do you know about Islam? The following site uses a cartoon to encourage discussion on stereotyping.

http://www.teachmideast.org/essays/26-stereotypes/38-stereotypes-of-arabs-middle-easterners-and-muslims

This site serves as a reminder that stereotypes are deeply entrenched in our history. African Americans, Jews, Latinos, Native peoples, and others have been wrapped into a package easily targeted for prejudice. When have you experienced prejudicial stereotyping? How did you react?

http://arabstereotypes.org/blog/201307/31-419

Colombia 1976

"Another Missionary Christmas Story"   p. 22

Discussion Theme: Globalization and Syncretism

1. Christmas trees are a significant part of many cultures. Do you know where the use of the Christmas tree actually began? A group member should come prepared to share the history of the Christmas tree, particularly in Germany.

2. Given the discussion of the history of the Christmas tree, strategize ways to make the Christmas tree a more effective religious teaching tool for your family and your church.

3. What are the pagan origins of the Christmas tree? Many Christians feel that anything that has a pagan origin should not be incorporated into the church. Identify valid points for that argument. What are the dangers of incorporating pagan practices into Christianity?

4. An important term for the church to understand during our rush to globalization is *syncretism*. Globalization is the process of standardizing ideas and commodities around the world. *Syncretism* is the blending of different forms of belief and practice into another faith. For example, many forms of meditation are being incorporated into Christian spirituality. Why could syncretism be of value to the local church? Why could it be a danger?

5. Jews and Christians are warned about the dangers of blending different religious and secular perspectives. "Do not add to what I command you and do not subtract from it, but keep the commands of the Lord your God that I give you" (Deuteronomy 4:2). "You shall have no other gods before me" (Exodus 20:3). "Do not be carried away by all kinds of strange teachings. It is good for our hearts to be strengthened by grace, not by eating ceremonial foods, which is of no benefit to those who do so" (Hebrews 13:9). Are those warnings relevant today? What spiritual teachings from other religions are being incorporated into contemporary Christianity?

6. What different nationalities are represented in your community? Think about restaurant owners, hotel owners, medical professionals, university professors and students, and other immigrants (legal and illegal). What do you think non-Christian immigrants do on Christian holidays? Have you ever considered inviting them to share your family's celebration of such special days? If you did invite them and they accepted, how would you go about sharing your faith during such a visit? What kind of statements or questions could you make or ask that would lead to the opportunity to share your faith?

7. Consider having your church host a specific event during a holiday

that would showcase the stories behind the holiday as a way to intentionally teach the meaning behind it. As Christians are we mandated to share our faith with unbelievers? Why or why not? Is the following verse a mandate or an option? "But you will receive power when the Holy Spirit comes on you; and you will be my witnesses in Jerusalem, and in all Judea and Samaria, and to the ends of the earth" (Acts 1:8). How many people in your church have accepted Christ in the last five years?

Activity Possibility—Developing a Holistic View of Missions

Missions involve a great deal of work. Broad mission action at the local church cannot occur without careful study, thoughtful planning, and thorough execution. The following websites provide reliable designs to assist pastors and mission team leaders in the development of a holistic view of missions that is appropriate for any given church.

http://www.davidmays.org/teambook.pdf

http://www.actsone8.com/prepare/

Colombia 1977

"Mi Familia Me Botó" ("My Family Threw Me Away")   p. 24

Discussion Theme: Forgiveness and Reconciliation

1. What experiences help you identify with the pain of a family entrapped by the bitterness of negative experiences that make forgiveness and reconciliation difficult? What kind of human frailties lead to broken relationships within families?

2. What is the difference between forgiveness and forgetting? Can a person forgive without forgetting? Why or why not?

3. What is the first thing you should do when alienated from another person? Why is God always willing to forgive? Read Psalm 103:8-12. How can "steadfast love" encourage forgiveness and reconciliation?

4. Explain whether you think resentment most hurts the person that

hosts it or the person being resented. Some studies show unresolved resentment as a precipitant for physical illnesses. What do you think might be the reason for such illness?

5. Study the following passages and select one that you would like to commit to memory to serve as a reminder of the importance of forgiveness—"For if you forgive men when they sin against you, your heavenly Father will also forgive you" (Matthew 6:14). "Who is a God like you, who pardons sin and forgives the transgression of the remnant of his inheritance? You do not stay angry forever but delight to show mercy. You will again have compassion on us; you will tread our sins underfoot and hurl all our iniquities into the depths of the sea" (Micah 7:18-19).

6. Is it possible to explore new relationships if reconciliation has not been achieved in former broken relationships? How could one affect the other?

Activity Possibility—Walking the Path of Reconciliation
This site explores three key elements in reconciliation.

http://lifesourceministries.info/2013/05/23/why-is-reconciliation-important/

Matthew 5:23-24 explores the importance of forgiveness as a prelude to worship.

http://discovertheword.org/2011/08/15/find-out-why-reconciliation-is-an-important-part-of-the-christian-life/

Colombia 1977

"Hot Air Balloons on a Bus"   p. 26

Discussion Theme: Fear and Faith
1. What are the usual responses to fear? What are the differences between rational and irrational fears? What are some rational fears? What are some irrational fears?

2. How did the missionary in this story react to his moment of fear? What kept him from succumbing to the natural emotions that accompany the loss of control?

3. Share with your study group some irrational fears with which you struggle. How do you cope with them? How have you overcome some irrational fears? Which fears keep you from doing things your really want to do?

4. How does fear handicap your effort to become more deeply involved in missions?

5. How does the Bible address the issue of fear? Give specific examples that involve the emotion of fear. Consider Jesus in Gethsemane and the story of Jonah's call and response.

6. Write a contemporary paraphrase of Jonah's call (Jonah 1:1-3) and insert your name and a specific place where you would most be afraid to be called. If called, could you buck up to the challenge and go? If not, what might be the realistic consequences of disobedience, other than being swallowed by a "large mouthed" fish?

Activity Possibility—Missions and Prayer

With what frequency do you and your church pray for missionaries? These websites might be good starting points.

http://www.wycliffe.org/pray/prayon/howtoprayfor/missionaries.aspx

http://www.whatchristianswanttoknow.com/10-prayers-for-missions-or-mission-trips/

Colombia 1978

"The Day Jaime Decided to Become a Missionary"   p. 32

Discussion Theme: Alcoholism and Missions

1. What do you think about the church being involved with alcoholics? What specifically is the role of the church in relation to

assisting alcoholics? What are some specific ministries that even the smallest church might offer? Why do most alcoholics avoid the church, or do they?

2. Where are Alcoholics Anonymous and Al-Anon meetings held in your area?

3. Do you think one person's consumption of alcohol encourages others to do likewise? If your drinking might lead another person alcoholism, would it make a difference in your attitude about social drinking?

4. Returning to the case of Jaime in the story, how could the pastor have ministered to Jaime?

5. The Bible has multiple warnings about the abuse of alcoholic drinks. Review Proverbs 4:17; 20:1; 23:19-20; 23:21; 23:29-30; and 23:31-35. What are the actual dangers of drunkenness?

Activity Possibility—Teaching English as a Second Language in Your Community

People in nearly every community lack the resources and funds to learn English despite the importance of that language for finding a job, communicating with neighbors, reading important notices or signs, etc. Therefore, these people face unnecessary injustices. Perhaps you or your church can help.

http://www.uni.edu/becker/TESOL_ESL2.html

https://owl.english.purdue.edu/owl/resource/586/01/

No Particular Place—Any Specific Time

"The Society for the Picking of Apples"   p. 36

Discussion Theme: **Jerusalem, Judah, Samaria, and the Ends of the Earth**

1. Why do you think Jesus chose to use the four locations he mentioned in Acts 1:8? "But you will receive power when the Holy

Spirit comes on you; and you will be my witnesses in Jerusalem, and in all Judea and Samaria, and to the ends of the earth."

2. If Jesus had centered his ministry in your city, what other locations would he likely have used in lieu of Judea, Samaria, and the ends of the earth? If you consider the four locations as your home city (Jerusalem), your state (Judah), a place no one wants to go (Samaria), and to the ends of the earth (a country other than the country of your birth), how might your church be involved in some way in all four areas of ministry? Create a written plan for this involvement.

3. How did Jesus' disciples take Acts 1:8 seriously in terms of where they eventually established ministries? The following site reviews the life of each apostle---http://www.biblepath.com/apostles.html.

Activity Possibility—The Biblical Basis of Missions

A mission strategy for the local church must be based on scriptural mandates rather than the personal opinions and interests of a church's leaders. The two websites below provide a reminder of key verses of scripture that provide the foundation for a responsible mission theology.

http://www.christianitytoday.com/edstetzer/2010/january/ten-scripture-texts-on-gods-mission.html

http://www.whatchristianswanttoknow.com/15-motivational-bible-verses-for-missions/

Colombia 1978

"Not Going to the Dogs"   p. 39

Discussion Theme: Is It Rational to Think Humans Can Have a Friendship with God?

1. Why do you believe God is interested in a friendship with you?

2. In what context does the Bible refer to God as a friend? Read John 15:15; James 2:23; and John 15:14.

3. Share with your study group an experience when God became real for you. Is this a frequent or infrequent event? How can you help other people begin to experience God as a friend?

4. What are the advantages of relating to God personally?

5. Review the hymn, "What a Friend We Have in Jesus." What is the message of the hymn?

6. Whom do you consider to be your best friend? What are the characteristics of that relationship? Could God qualify for the role of best friend? Why or why not?

Activity Possibility—Adopt a Missionary

The following links include helpful guidelines for congregations interested in direct support of missionaries. Although they suggest specific missionaries, the same principles of support are valid for any denomination or individual wanting to support a missionary from your congregation or denomination.

http://international.sojournchurch.com/?page_id=2899

http://www.ccminternational.org/English/perspective/Adopt%20a%20Missionary.htm

U.S.A. 1979

"Emmaus Road Experience"   p. 44

Discussion Theme: **Spiritual Understanding and Interpretation**
Read Luke 24:13-35.

1. Spiritual perception is the ability to recognize the "hand" of God in life. In what ways do you make a daily effort to recognize God's initiatives to guide your life?

2. What was the obstacle that kept the father from seeing his son?

3. What are the similarities between this story and the biblical account in Luke 24?

4. How do you understand the role of a spiritual advisor? Who are spiritual advisors in your community? How would it be helpful for you to meet with someone periodically to help you plot a strategy for your personal spiritual growth? Perhaps you could invite a spiritual advisor to your session to explain spiritual direction.

5. Have you considered offering your services to mentor a new Christian as he or she begins his or her walk with Jesus? If so, where could you get further preparation? There is a plethora of books on discipling; one such book is *Organic Discipleship* by Dennis McCallum and Jessica Lowery.

Activity Possibility—The Emmaus Walk

Many denominations and para-church groups have developed exciting programs to guide individuals toward a more personal relationship with Christ. These programs provide valuable tools and training for strengthening the membership of the church. You might consider inviting a person that has participated in an Emmaus walk to speak to your group.

http://emmaus.upperroom.org

http://www.socalemmaus.org/Explanation_Of_Emmaus.htm

U.S.A. 1980

Read "The Child's Mite"   p. 45

Discussion Theme: Missions and Money

1. How much money would you have to give to a mission project of your choice to actually feel the financial strain of making a sacrifice? Have you ever given to that extent?

2. Luke 21:1-4 tells a story about a poor widow. What do you speculate happened to the lady who gave her last dime to others? Does God expect us to give to the point of destitution?

3. How might you contribute to missions in a non-financial way? Consider providing a gift-in-kind, such as working at food kitchen,

or working for Habitat for Humanity.

4. Discuss the validity of the statement, "All persons should give some of their financial resources to assist with missions."

5. If your church spends all of its income on itself, should you use a portion of your personal tithe or offerings to support missions through another organization? Why or why not?

6. How could your study group or you be a mission advocate to help your church explore the giving of more money to mission efforts outside the local church?

7. List five activities your study group could do to raise money to support one individual missionary, i.e. a bake sale, a pancake breakfast, or a church wide garage sale.

Activity Possibility—Addressing Community Needs

Sometimes it is helpful to review the variety of mission organizations that meet community needs around the world. Maybe the purpose of one of these organizations will be an incentive for you to get involved in some type of mission service. The following link lists a large number of mission agencies and provides a brief description of the focus of each one.

http://www.beesondivinity.com/missionsagencies

The following non-denomination link maintains a database of mission opportunities and a catalog of mission resources. This site is helpful when your church or denomination doesn't provide opportunities to match your skill or calling.

http://www.missionfinder.org

U.S.A. 1980

"The Conversion of a Dump"   p. 46

Discussion Theme: Conversion and Sanctification

1. Based on the words of Jesus found in the Bible, what would you say was his mission statement? Some possibilities are: "I am the

way"..."Love your neighbor as yourself"..."Father, forgive them"..."Blessed are"..."I am the Light of the World."

2. One church has as its mission statement—"Reaching as Many People for Christ as Soon as Possible." Why is this a good mission statement?

3. What are the key components of a mission statement?

4. What is the value of a mission statement if it is woven into the planning, execution, and evaluation of a church program?

5. What is your church's mission statement? How can it be strengthened?

Activity Possibility—Writing a Mission Statement

If your church or study group is struggling with the development of a mission statement, the following website will provide assistance.

http://www.missionstatements.com/church_mission_statements.html

China 1980

"Where Should We Evangelize?"   p. 47

Discussion Theme: **Strategy, Freedom, and Audacity**

1. This story focuses on the irony that we agonize about the lack of freedom in some parts of the world, rather than the freedom we fail to use in our own country. A distinct difference exists between the freedom to share your faith in the United States and China. How do you go about sharing your faith with an unbeliever? How do you take advantage of your freedom of expression in your country that you would be unable to do in China?

2. Acts 7 records one of the most audacious sermons in Christian history! The sermon focuses on telling some of the stories of God's faithfulness with the Jews and their unwillingness to reciprocate with obedience. What would you share if you knew it was the last sermon or speech you would utter on earth?

3. What are your reasons for not talking to your friends about faith?

4. Why is talking about your favorite sport, children, or spouse easier than talking about your God?

5. Would you like to be trained about how to share your faith?

6. What would you say or do if a stranger came up to you and said, "What do I need to do to become a Christian?" After a discussion of the question, divide your group in pairs and experiment with responding to that question.

7. Is anyone in your group familiar with the "Four Spiritual Laws"? The leader should come to the group session prepared to explain them and their value as an evangelistic tool. They have long been used as an evangelistic tool by Campus Crusade and may be found at: http://www.campuscrusade.com/fourlawseng.htm

8. Have you ever led anyone to Christ? How did it happen? How important is audacity in sharing your faith?

9. Who was instrumental in leading you to Christ? How did that happen?

Activity Possibility—Tools for Personal Evangelism

Not every evangelistic tool is effective for every person. The key is to saturate yourself with methods so that when an opportunity to share the importance of faith arises, the Holy Spirit will be able to draw from your memory what is necessary for the person to hear the greatest story ever told. The following link offer numerous suggestions for sharing your faith.

http://www.wheaton.edu/BGC/Equipping-Corner/Personal-Evangelism-Tools

U.S.A. 1980

"Could Prayer Be the Only Answer?"   p. 48

Discussion Theme: **Missions and Miracles**

1. Do you believe in miracles? How do you define a miracle?

2. How frequently does the Bible mention miracles?

3. What miracles have you witnessed?

4. Can you accept the reality of supernatural events even though you have never personally witnessed them? Is such acceptance what we call faith? What do we mean by "blind" faith?

5. John 6:1-15 records Jesus feeding the multitude. A version of this miracle is found in all four Gospels, unlike most other miracles. Why do you think all four writers deemed this miracle important? Have you ever been so hungry you hoped for a miracle? Why do you think Jesus also mentioned food in the Lord's Prayer? How involved in issues related to hunger should the church be? How is your church addressing the need?

6. Many Christians say, "The Bible is the absolute authority for my faith and practice." What does that statement mean to you?

7. If the Bible is your authority for faith and practice, what does that say about accepting the validity of miracles?

8. Do you believe the experience described in today's story was a miracle, a special event, a coincidence, or a non-miraculous answer to prayer? Why?

Activity Possibility—The Role of Prayer in Missions

The following website by Pittsburg Theological Seminary offers numerous power point programs. The last program on the list gives an abundance of discussion material concerning "Concerts of Prayer." "Concerts of Prayer" describe the idea of a gathering for an extraordinary focus on prayer.

http://www.worldmissioninitiative.org/index.php/resources/mission-education

http://powertochange.com/experience/spiritual-growth/prayerquotes/

Colombia 1982

"Should I or Shouldn't I?"   p. 50

Discussion Theme: **The Value of Mission Trips**
Have you considered taking a mission trip to another state or country?

1. Does the commitment of Mr. Nicks inspire you to try to find a similar project?

2. In Mark 6:7-12, Jesus sends his disciples in teams. What do you make of Jesus sending people to minister in teams of two? What is the advantage of teams as compared to individuals?

3. What talents do you have that could be useful to people who have recently had their home destroyed by an earthquake? Such skills include: carpenter, painter, plumber, electrician, agriculture specialist, cook, administrator, travel logistics coordinator, Bible study leader, preacher, gofer, teacher, fund raiser, musician, prayer warrior, social worker, and counselor.

4. Could you put together a mission team from your study group and/or their spouses to gut and rebuild a burned-out church kitchen in rural Appalachia? What teammates, with gifts not in your current group, would you need to recruit?

5. Are you familiar with an individual who frequently coordinates mission trips that might be able to mentor your group in mission trip planning? Does your denomination provide such a service?

6. What do you think it would cost to sponsor one person from your church for a stateside or international trip? Expenses include transportation, lodging, supplies, and food.

Activity Possibility—Deploy an International Volunteer

The following two secular websites offer international volunteer opportunities for a variety of occupations in many countries.

http://www.idealist.org/info/IntlVolunteer/Program

http://www.goabroad.com/volunteer-abroad

Colombia 1983

"The Eye of the Tiger"   p. 53

Discussion Theme: **Going Where You Have Never Gone**

1. This story illustrates the adventure and advantage of pushing the envelope just a little bit in one's life. When a little danger is involved in Christian service, how do you normally react? If you fight through the fear, what spiritual tools do you use?

2. Do you think a mission trip to a homeless shelter in a dangerous area of the inner city would raise your anxiety level? How do you cope with those kinds of fears to serve people who need you?

3. Paul's missionary journeys included a certain amount of reason for fear. If you had been Paul's mother or father, how would you have reacted to his call to carry the gospel around the world? "Three times I was beaten with rods, once I was pelted with stones, three times I was shipwrecked, I spent a night and a day in the open sea, I have been constantly on the move. I have been in danger from rivers, in danger from bandits, in danger from my fellow Jews, in danger from Gentiles; in danger in the city, in danger in the country, in danger at sea; and in danger from false believers. I have labored and toiled and have often gone without sleep; I have known hunger and thirst and have often gone without food; I have been cold and naked" (2 Corinthians 11:25-27).

4. What community activity could your group plan that would stretch your desire to do something of a "servant" nature that you have never done? Make a list of five possibilities.

Activity Possibility—The Need for an Understanding of Islam and other Religions in Order to Defend Christianity

Do you understand the meaning of *apologetics*? Simply defined, religious apologetics is the logical defense of a theological position. The following sites are helpful when studying about the differences between Christianity and other religions. All Christians should be informed and able to defend their faith in discussion with believers of other religions. As noted before, this study guide does not endorse everything written in these suggested web resources; they are provided to encourage study, reflection, and discussion.

http://answering-islam.org/index.html

http://carm.org/religious-movements/islam/methods-muslims-use-attack-christianity

Ecuador 1983

"The Pitfalls of Prosperity"   p. 56

Discussion Theme: Understanding Poverty

1. The writer of this story was obviously feeling guilt due to the disparity between his wealth and his friend's poverty. Does such disparity trouble you? Why?

2. What causes you to think about the economic disparity between families in your community? Why should a Christian give prayerful thought to this subject? Note the biblical insights: "In everything I did, I showed you that by this kind of hard work we must help the weak, remembering the words the Lord Jesus himself said: 'It is more blessed to give than to receive'" (Acts 20:35). "Give to the one who asks you, and do not turn away from the one who wants to borrow from you" (Matthew 5:42).

3. Measuring wealth between two families is always relative. Given what you can discern from the small amount of information about the friendship in today's story, what would you have done if you were the wealthy individual in the story? Why do you think Julieta felt guilt rather than resentment?

4. Speaking honestly, how do you usually make decisions—based on

what is practically better for you or on what the Bible encourages in terms of assisting the poor?

5. What does the Bible say about how people of faith should try to balance economic inequality?

6. Do you think it is true that poor people are actually happier than wealthier people? What is your rationale for such a belief?

7. If you could do one thing tomorrow for a person in financial need, what would it be? Will you commit to doing it?

Activity Possibility—Your Wealth Quotient

Based on your net worth, make a guess as to where you sit in comparison to the rest of the world in terms of percentage—top ten percent, top fifty percent, etc. Chances are you will be surprised.

http://www.globalrichlist.com/wealth

https://www.hopevault.org/rank.php

U.S.A. 1990

"Respecting the Seventh Generation"   p. 57

Discussion Theme: Cultural Sensitivity

1. Cultural sensitivity can be discussed from two perspectives. First, do we understand the perspective of cultures other than our own? Second, is our culture sensitive to issues such as ecumenicity, gender, the environment, etc.? Common courtesy demands that that individuals respect cultures different from their own.

2. North Americans are accused of being unconcerned about what is going on outside their own country. How do you feel about that statement?

3. Many people from a variety of cultures try to leave their countries? If you lived in an oppressive country, would you flee?

4. Thinking about tourists, what actions of foreign tourists really tick

you off? Are you especially sensitive when traveling so that you are not guilty of being accused of being an "Ugly American," "Ugly Japanese," or "Ugly South Korean?"

5. If you are going to travel internationally, how do you prepare? Other countries can be sensitive about the pictures you take as well as the behavior you exhibit. What do you know about the country's history and current politics?

6. Reflecting about the story for today, when you make a decision about the environment, how do you consider the implications upon future generations? For example, do you see any reason to recycle on a regular basis?

7. The question is really not whether there is or is not global warming! The issue is whether you try to do your share to protect the environment for future generations. What do you do that requires a special effort to protect the environment?

Activity Possibility—Caring for Missionaries

First-term missionaries often do not survive their first term; fifteen percent of them burn out and resign. The following sites offer ways you and your church can provide support for missionaries before, during, and after their service.

http://www.missionarycare.com/ebook.htm#mmcintro

http://www.missionarycare.com/links.htm

Colombia 1991—2013

"The Power of Unity within the Body of the Church"   p. 58

Discussion Theme: **Doing Together What We Can't Do Alone**

1. Are you more comfortable working by yourself or as a team? Why?

2. What mission projects are more appropriate for an individual than a group?

3. What specific mission project could your study group undertake?

Have you ever written a missionary to request a list of ways your church could assist in his or her ministry? Draft such a letter and send it to a missionary whom one of your group knows.

4. What mission project do you (or your church) have that is uniquely your own? What is it? How does it help to reach people for Christ?

5. What could you do specifically, by yourself, for a missionary that often goes undone?

6. Today's story is a unique example of the value of a lot of Christians working together to achieve a purpose that no one person could accomplish. What would have happened if one link in this chain of cooperation had not responded positively when the need arose?

7. Is it possible to be a part of a Christian mission project without being a Christian? Related to the story, are doctors obligated to be Christian to participate in "Project Smile?"

Activity Possibility—Using a Church Mission Profile

Your church can benefit from using a mission profile to evaluate your current program.

http://www.cartpioneers.org/content/MissionsAssessmentProfile.pdf

The following sound bite notes ten ways to evaluate your mission program.

http://www.themissionsociety.org/learn/multimedia/medialib/media-templ/article/48435

China 1991

"The Impossible Made Tangible"   p. 61

Discussion Theme: Expanding Your Worldview

1. What is the meaning of *provincialism*? In what ways is *provincialism* compatible with Christianity?

2. Do you thing God has a bias in favor for any particular nation? Why or why not? Obviously, the Old Testament describes the Jews as

God's chosen people. Did that change with the arrival of the Messiah? How can you justify that position based on the scriptures of the New Testament?

3. How do you define *global worldview*? What do you think of the idea that it is better to pray "God bless the world" instead of "God bless America?"

4. Two scriptures come to mind about God's inclusiveness. "Then Peter began to speak: 'I now realize how true it is that God does not show favoritism.'" (Acts 10:1-35, particularly verse 34). And, "There is neither Jew nor Gentile, neither slave nor free, nor is there male and female, for you are all one in Christ Jesus" (Galatians 3:28). What is your understanding of the phrase, "God shows no favoritism." How does that change the way you look at certain nationalities?

5. To understand today's story, how much do you need to know about the history of China?

6. If you are striving to be a "prayer warrior," is it important to keep aware of international news? How effectively can you witness to a friend from another country if you know nothing about his or her country? How important is such knowledge in terms of opening the doors to a friendship with an immigrant or a visitor to your country?

Activity Possibility—Missionary Profiles from the Past
It is beneficial to become acquainted with the wealth of inspiration by reading missionary biographies.

http://urbana.org/go-and-do/missionary-biographies

http://www.missionarybiographies.com

Africa 1991

"Just Getting There and Home Is a Mission in Itself"   p. 63

Discussion Theme: **What Do You Know about Africa?**
1. The Internet has opened up the world to everyone who wants to be exposed to places where they have never been. Whether your favorite missionary is in a country in Africa, Asia, or South America, you can become better informed about the country by spending a few hours in front of your computer. Browse the internet to find answers to the following questions. What is the weather in Harare, Tanzania today?

2. What is the lead news for Harare?

3. What is the currency, time, and electrical system in Harare?

4. Could you take a safari while visiting missionaries in Tanzania?

5. Is Harare a dangerous location to visit?

6. What are the best tourist sites around Harare?

7. Are there "Unreached People Groups" in Tanzania?

8. What mission agencies are working in Tanzania? Does your denomination work in Tanzania or other countries in Africa?

9. What would it cost for a round-trip plane fare to Harare?

Activity Possibility—Mission Fair or Conference
Traditionally, the local church has found a fair or conference to be a beneficial tool to increase mission awareness. With creativity, it can still work.

http://www.anniearmstrong.com/anniearmstrongpb.aspx?pageid=13639

http://fim.org/sites/fim.org/files/Missions%20Conference%20Themes.pdf

China 1991

"Blood-Stained Glory"   p. 68

Discussion Theme: **Civil Disobedience**
1. Civil disobedience is rarely discussed in the church. What is civil

disobedience? Why is it such an "untouchable" subject in the church?

2. When have you felt that a law in your state or country was unjust? How did you react? What measures did you take?

3. Identify a biblical example of civil disobedience. In those cases, how did God respond to the disobedience of the faithful?

4. Discuss the pros and cons of a group protest to foment civil reform in China or your own country.

5. Have you ever been involved in civil disobedience?

6. Could Jesus have been accused of civil disobedience? When and why?

7. Every country experiences key historical events that could be considered fundamental in its march toward freedom. What are the three most important events in the formation of your country's freedom? What role did the church play in those three events?

8. What is your position on the separation of church and state? Is your position compatible with your theology?

Activity Possibility—Human Trafficking

Few Christians realize the extent of human trafficking. Take a look at the statistics related to pornography—a primary driving force funding human trafficking.

http://www.youtube.com/watch?v=fVXf_MrekHw

http://www.state.gov/j/tip/rls/tiprpt/2013/210546.htm

U.S.A. 1993

"A Mission Challenge" p. 71

Discussion Theme: The Importance of Mission Goals

1. What specific goals related to missions does your church have? Do

you think your church should have written goals? How do you evaluate whether the church is succeeding in missions?

2. Experts say goals should be measureable, meaningful, and attainable. How well do your goals and those of your church meet this criteria?

3. Write three goals for your study group concerning a missionary family that meet those three specific standards.

4. Write three goals about activities your study group could do to provide financial support for a missionary salary or a specific mission project.

Activity Possibility—Mission Quotes

Group members are encouraged to advocate for the use of mission quotes on church websites, in bulletins or newsletters, bulletin boards, etc. Allow the following mission quotations to fire your commitment to missions.

http://www.whatchristianswanttoknow.com/22-awesome-quotes-for-mission-trips-and-missionaries/

http://www.proverbs2525.org/collections/quotes_missions.php

Macau 1993

"The Gift of Hospitality"   p. 74

Discussion Theme: Using Hospitality for Evangelism

1. How do you define *hospitality*?

2. Who do you know who has the gift of hospitality? Who in your church really enjoys entertaining people in his or her home?

3. How could you team with a person who has the gift of hospitality to use your gift of encouragement, evangelism, music, or teaching? For example, what if you teamed to invite internationals into one of your homes and initiated a friendship that might lead to being able to share the gospel?

4. What would be the advantages of entertained missionaries in your home and invited your children and grandchildren to enjoy the evening of fellowship?

5. What if your church invited an international from the country where a missionary serves to attend a presentation by that missionary with the understanding that they would be asked to respond positively or negatively to the presentation?

6. What strategy do you have to create an opportunity to share your faith? The joy and effectiveness of faith sharing comes with experience and evaluation of each effort. The greatest comfort is the reality that the Holy Spirit will use our evangelistic effort to God's glory.

7. How would you feel about inviting a Buddhist or a Moslem to talk about their country, customs, and spirituality over a meal in your home?

8. Being deeply honest, how much do you care whether people of other faiths hear about Jesus Christ? If a person of another faith approached you and asked you to explain Christianity, what would you tell them?

Activity Possibility—Faith Sharing
The following websites provide ample material to direct a thoughtful discussion of the importance of faith-sharing.

https://www.unlockingthebible.org/afraid-to-share-your-faith/

http://www.biblewriter.com/witness.htm

Japan 1995

"Giving Back"   p. 77

Discussion Theme: **How Do You Spend Your Money?**
(This subject may be a very sensitive one for public discussion.) It is often said that if you study a person's check stubs, you can learn a lot about his

or her priorities. How true that is!

1. The Bible speaks about a metaphorical term not known to many—*the offering of the first fruits.* "As soon as the order went out, the Israelites generously gave the first fruits of their grain, new wine, olive oil and honey and all that the fields produced. They brought a great amount, a tithe of everything (2 Chronicles 31:5). What is the meaning of this term? Is this concept also found in the New Testament? What would one suppose is the difference in an apple given from the first of the harvest and one given from the last of the harvest? How does that concept relate to when you write your check to the church or other benevolent causes?

2. Since this is a study of missions, how regularly do you financially support missionaries or mission efforts?

How Does Your Church Spend Its Money?

3. If your church does not have a budget, what does that say about the stewardship of the church? Are your contributions based only on covering the necessary expenses of the local church? How interested are your church leaders in challenging the church's membership to give more in order to serve the community and the world?

4. What percentage of your church budget goes to mission outreach?

5. Does your church budget have specific line items for the four categories of mission giving highlighted in Acts 1:8: missions in your community, missions in your state/country, missions to people generally ignored by the church, and missions to unreached people?

6. When did your church last increase its mission giving?

Activity Possibility—Regifting for the Benefit of Missions

Many individuals and churches use regifting as a way to enhance mission giving, the following two links may be helpful for your group to donate more money to missions because of spending less on expensive gifts.

http://www.regiftable.com/Regifting101/

The following webpage outlines ten rules to guide the practice of regifting.

http://www.daveramsey.com/blog/10-rules-of-regifting

Russian Republics 1995

"Using the Cultural Decorum for Faith Purposes" p. 77

Discussion Theme: **How Do Missionaries Raise Their Financial Support?**

1. Generally speaking there are two ways to fund missionaries: some missionaries are salaried by their denomination, while others are required to raise their own support from donor churches or individuals. Discuss the differences between the two structures. What are the advantages and disadvantage of each? How does your church support its missionaries?

2. How much time does it take an average missionary family to raise the needed financial support? How is the needed level/amount of support determined?

3. What makes some people better than others at raising funds? How do you feel when you receive a request to contribute to a missionary's support? What difference does it make if the missionary is talking with you or your congregation in person as opposed to receiving a written request for financial support?

4. Many couples who feel called to the mission field are unable to go because they cannot secure the necessary money. Look for statistics on the Internet regarding the percentage of missionaries who fail to raise support. Why do you think some people are unable to raise the needed support?

5. If you believe it is important for people, like those mentioned in today's story, to be exposed to the good news of Jesus Christ, how

will that happen without the sending of missionaries? How can you support missionaries other than with financial assistance?

6. Does your church contribute directly to a missionary's support? Why or why not? What could you do to initiate or raise your church's support for missionaries?

Activity Possibility—Study Mission Hymns

The group leader might select three unfamiliar mission hymns from the sites below and bring the lyrics for the group to study. The Holy Spirit could ignite a new mission spirit through such a study.

http://home.snu.edu/~hculbert/classics.htm

http://www.sharefaith.com/guide/Christian-Music/hymns-the-songs-and-the-stories/articles.html

Colombia 2000

"God Spoke Very Loudly Here"   p. 79

Discussion Theme: **The Possibilities of a Mission Trip**

1. Have you ever been a part of mission team that was formed to assist in an area recently devastated by a crisis? Where did you serve? What was your role?

2. If members of your church have been involved in such a trip, invite them to attend this session to share some of their experiences.

3. How does your pastor or mission team keep you aware of opportunities to serve on such teams?

4. What is the most recent disaster (earthquake, bombing, tornado, fire, etc.) within driving distance of your church? What would be involved in planning a work trip for your group? Imagine that you have ten people wanting to serve as a work team to assist with clean up from a tornado 100 miles from your church. Spend fifteen minutes making a quick list of the logistics necessary for such as a trip: recruitment of members, connection with an agency already

working on the ground, estimate of cost, transportation, purpose, prayer team, work description, etc.

5. In the story for today, David felt more vulnerable before God in a foreign land with unknown team members, and working with people in need. Why do you think this is true?

6. How does God speak to you? Where do you feel most likely to hear God's voice? When was the last time you God spoke to you?

Activity Possibility—Organize or Participate in a Mission Trip

The following site provides suggestions concerning trip preparation, team preparation, departure, and return.

http://missiontriptools.com

Most denominations and other organizations have websites that provide ideas for the different phases of short-term mission trips. The following is one of many.

https://home.snu.edu/~hculbert/short.htm

Colombia 2000

"A Friend Sent Me"   p. 82

Discussion Theme: "Here Am I, Send Me"

1. Read Isaiah 6:8. "Then I heard the voice of the Lord saying, 'Whom shall I send? And who will go for us?' And I said, 'Here am I. Send me!'"

2. Many people respond to God's call to serve outside their culture, whether short or long-term. Give people in your group the opportunity to speak about their "calling." How did it happen? What was the objective of the call?

3. The giver of crosses evidently planned to use them as a form of witness during the mission trip. Do you have a strategy to witness?

4. Have you ever been privileged to be the person God used to lead a

person accept Christ? Share something about that experience.

5. What is your opinion of scripture tracts? Have you ever used one? What stories have you heard about people coming to Christ because they read a tract in a moment of need? In what situations might tracts serve as a valuable evangelistic tool?

Activity Possibility—Monitoring Natural Crises around the Globe
Churches and individuals with financial resources beyond their personal needs are greatly blessed when they open their hearts to the needs of others. If we know about international crises, we are more likely to respond to needs. Here are two good sights that publicize recent global crisis.

http://globaldisasterwatch.blogspot.com

http://www.gdacs.org

Brazil 2004

"On a Rock in a Hard Spot" p. 83

Discussion Theme: **Writing Your Testimony in the Form of a Story**

1. Read the testimony on p. 83 and also the suggested steps for writing a story on pages 112-116 in *God's Mighty Acts Around the Globe*. Much of today's session will be spent reading and writing with the belief that telling your story is the best way to witness to an unbeliever.

2. Have you ever written a story as a way to communicate your testimony in a non-obtrusive way?

3. What experience in your life most convinced you that God wants to interact with you? Give the group fifteen minutes to write a brief testimonial story.

4. Share your stories one with another. This may be the first time that some members have shared their testimony. No story should be critiqued or questioned.

Activity Possibility—Story Writing and Story Telling

Many articles in most mission periodicals are stories of personal experiences. Your story may be worthy of publication. Check out some mission stories in "Mission Frontiers."

http://www.missionfrontiers.org/issue/current

One of the best ways to master storytelling is by listening to good storytellers. Moth is a company that promotes storytelling. They provide podcasts of storytelling events on a variety of subjects from across the country. The site is incredibly entertaining and often inspirational.

http://themoth.org/stories

Myanmar 2004

"On the Roads of Mandalay"   p. 86

Discussion Theme: **International Awareness**
(The leader of the discussion group will need to do some investigation in preparation for this class)

1. How excited would your church be about adopting a country as a mission focus? What would your group think about setting a goal of becoming more informed about a particular country than any other person in your community?

2. Select Myanmar (Burma) as your country (or a different country of your choice.) What can you learn on Wikipedia about the country?

3. Where is it located? Who are famous citizens of the country?

4. What is the status of Myanmar's religious freedom? Do any Burmese live in your city that you could invite to your session?

5. How can you pray effectively for the people of Myanmar?

6. Who is Adoniron Judson? What made Judson so important in relation to Myanmar? The leader of the group should come prepared to speak about Judson's biography. Do you know any

missionaries who have worked in Myanmar?

Activity Possibility: Suggested Mission Books

Mission advocates should read one missionary biography and another quality mission book annually. The following site lists some of the best resources.

https://missionbooks.org

Dominican Republic 2005

"The Least People of the World"   p. 89

Discussion Theme: **Uncomfortable Issues for the Church**

1. In today's story, the government of the Dominican Republic built a high wall to hide the social problems of their country. How many of the social issues mentioned are ones your church could address?

2. Let's look at a few of the problems, one at a time. What percentage of people in your community, town, or city regularly face hunger? What is your church doing to address this need in a measureable way?

3. We take pure water for granted. Ask your group to discuss if they use a sizeable amount of their income for bottled water. How much money do they estimate they spend on bottled water monthly? Why do you think people in your community use bottled water? Is it necessary? How willing would they be to give up the bottled water and instead donate the money to build a well or wells in a country with a water crisis? Is a Christian morally obligated to ask such a question? Why or why not?

4. Where are criminals incarcerated in your city? How do you feel about visiting a jail? Why? If other churches or organizations are already engaged in such a ministry, explore the possibility of joining with them. Invite someone with experience in jail ministry to speak to your church as a way for your membership to consider this type of ministry.

5. In biblical times, people with leprosy were ostracized from their families and communities. With what diseases or conditions do we see this happening today? How do you feel about working with these groups of people?

Activity Possibility—Worship and Mission for the Global Church

Although this activity does not relate to the discussion theme, it merits discussion as a mission concern. Churches need to appreciate and generate culturally appropriate worship for our changing world. Such change comes slowly, but it is possible as churches adjust to changing communities.

http://www.gbod.org/lead-your-church/multicultural-global-worship/resource/global-resources-for-worship-a-bibliography

The following link is a one-hour YouTube presentation on multi-cultural worship. This presentation could easily lead to four discussion sessions to discuss the theme adequately.

http://www.youtube.com/watch?v=lQj255F9Pal

U.S.A. 2005

"Recognizing God's Involvement in Your Life"   p. 91

Discussion Theme: Hearing the Quiet or Loud Voice of God

1. "The word of the Lord came to Jonah son of Amittai: 'Go to the great city of Nineveh and preach against it, because its wickedness has come up before me.' Jonah ran away from the Lord and headed for Tarshish. He went down to Joppa, where he found a ship bound for that port. After paying the fare, he went aboard and sailed for Tarshish to flee from the Lord" (Jonah 1:1-3).

2. In what situations are you most likely to hear the voice of God? Is it audible or inaudible? Is it frequent or infrequent?

3. What was Jonah's response when God ask him to go to Nineveh?

4. What do you think makes God's voice or God's presence so disturbing for most people? What specifically made Jonah so

uncomfortable? Why do you think mission callings are generally uncomfortable?

5. Where are you most likely to hear God's voice? Where do you go or what do you do (i. e., Jonah's Nineveh) to avoid giving God a chance to speak to you?

Activity Possibility—Journaling

One of the best ways to recognize and remember God's interaction with you is journaling. This daily discipline causes the writer to reflect upon the day in an effort to see and describe the personal relationship between him/herself and God.

http://home.earthlink.net/~haywoodm/SpiritualJournal.html

http://michaelhyatt.com/daily-journal.html

Mongolia 2006

"Giving Away What You Would Like to Keep!"   p. 92

Discussion Theme: **Mission Stewardship**

1. Define stewardship. Is the word *stewardship* used in the Bible? Using a concordance, find and read two passages on stewardship from the book of Proverbs.

2. Why do people usually associate stewardship with money?

3. What are different kinds of stewardship?

4. How does setting a monetary goal for a mission goal increase the possibility that more people will give generously?

5. When have you given away something you wanted to keep? Give group members the opportunity to share their stories. How did that gift affect the recipient? When have you seen generosity be contagious?

Activity Possibility—Raising Money for Missions

Some churches believe they have limited funds, but there are a host of ways to support mission church financially. Creative thinking is the solution. The web is full of imaginative ways to assist missionaries, underwrite projects, or fund mission trips. Visit these links to find some suggestions.

https://home.snu.edu/~hculbert/funds2.htm

http://globalyoungpeople.org/grants-scholarship/25-ways-to-raise-funds/

Mongolia 2006

"Where Two or Three Gather"   p. 95

Discussion Theme: **Church Development beyond Your Local Church**

1. How has your church been involved with the beginning of another church?

2. Why might a church outside the walls of the traditional church have more appeal to un-churched people? Would your congregation be open to sponsoring such a congregation? Maybe the high school and college students of your congregation could begin a store-front congregation near a school in your city. Or, you could begin a lunch Bible study near an area with a high traffic of businesswomen or men.

3. If your church is blessed with bi-lingual members, what are the possibilities of them starting a service in a language other than the one that is predominant in your community?

4. How open would your congregation be to starting a Friday night church to minister to people who often travel or work on Saturday and Sunday?

5. Is you church overlooking sub-groups in your city? The incarcerated, unwed mothers, the homeless, migrant workers, R.V. camps, and truckers are just a few.

6. Which group would be the best one upon which for your group to focus?

Activity Possibility—Discipleship of New Believers

Occasionally, new converts in a church are left to fend for themselves, which is unfortunate and often leads to discouragement. Here are suggestions to disciple new believers.

http://evangelism.intervarsity.org/how/discipleship/10-ways-disciple-brand-new-christians

South Korea and Afghanistan 2008

"How Will God Work Out This Tragedy?"   p. 97

Discussion Theme: A Missionary's Responsibility to the Larger Community

1. Good intentions do not always produce positive results. When you reflect on the experience of the South Korean missionaries mentioned in today's story, do you feel the decision by a church to commission missionaries to serve in a highly dangerous area was prudent? Why or why not?

2. If missionaries only went to friendly environments, how would the message of salvation reach those living in countries such as Afghanistan, Iraq, or North Korea?

3. Do you think a missionary's home country should be responsible for the safety of a missionary working in a dangerous environment?

4. If a ransom is paid to secure the freedom of a kidnapped missionary, what are the consequences of such a decision? How might the payment of one ransom lead to additional kidnappings?

5. How would you deal with a calling to serve in a country unfriendly to Christianity,?

6. What would be your response to a child or grandchild being called to the mission field? How would that differ from a child or grandchild being called to minister in your own country?

Activity Possibility—Promote Missions with Photos and Videos
We know a picture is better than a host of words. However, not all pictures

communicate a mission experience clearly. If you plan to illustrate a mission trip or a sermon to stimulate mission interest, take the time to learn to take captivating and motivating photos. One poignant verbal presentation is much more powerful than a long series of bad pictures.

http://blog.stanleyleary.com/2011/12/new-church-and-well-being-built-in.html

http://digital-photography-school.com/10-ways-to-take-stunning-portraits

Central Asia 2009

"Door #1, Door #2, or Door #3"   p. 100

Discussion Theme: **Creative Evangelism**

1. When the word *evangelism* is mentioned, who comes to mind as someone with whom you should share the gospel? If no one comes to mind, is it because you know no unbelievers or because you do not feel any responsibility to share the gospel with unbelievers?

2. This study book was written with the hope and expectation that readers would think about which of the stories might speak to friends and family.

3. What story about God working in your life could you use as an evangelism tool? One good strategy is to say, "I would like to share an experience with you and ask for your opinion of the experience." You then share the story and say, "Do you think God was involved in this experience?" If they say "No," you can then say, "Can I share my interpretation of the event?"

4. Allow members of your group to share creative ways to talk to people about Jesus and what they have to offer people that other religions do not have.

Activity Possibility—Unreached People Groups

Do you know the meaning of *unreached people groups*? The following sites will bring you up to speed. The websites for this story focus on the Joshua Project—the most extensive project to spread the gospel to unreached peoples. However, the second site focuses on how individuals can get involved. Don't miss these sites.

http://www.joshuaproject.net

http://www.joshuaproject.net/mission-ideas-for-individuals.php

U.S.A. 2009
"It's Amazing Who Celebrates Christmas"   p. 101
Discussion Theme: Creativity and Missions

1. All people have a degree of creativity. How does your creativity manifest itself? Some possibilities might be: carpentry, writing, painting, acting, or storytelling.

2. Make a list of other ways people express their creativity.

3. Discuss the universal ability to dream. How are dreams an effort of the mind to express creative screen writing?

4. Discuss the theology of creativity. Or, in other words, how does God relate to creation in terms of people's creativity?

5. The story for today is unique in the sense that a group of musically creative people used entertainment as a form of subtle evangelism. When have you seen or experienced the Holy Spirit through music? Allow time for group members to share.

6. How could you use your creative skills to bring glory to God?

7. One simple example is: "How can you decorate your house so it will bring glory to God?" What one key decoration for your home could you put on your most visible wall to draw attention and give you an opportunity to witness to your faith?"

Activity Possibility—Organizing an International Community Celebration

Today's story illustrates the opportunities to share the Gospel with people that have immigrated to your country. It is difficult to share your faith with your international neighbors unless you intentionally structure a way to get to know them. Your church could sponsor an international food fest, international art fair, or an international folk dance festival. Ideas from the following websites could be easily adapted for your church.

http://ualr.edu/programsabroad/home/get-involved-on-campus/international-celebration-week/

http://www.shu.edu/news/article/463113#.UmuyRxY_b4R

Israel 2012

"A Quiet Dove"   p. 102

Discussion Theme: **Remembering Your Baptism**
1. How do you understand the relationship between God and a person who is being baptized?

2. At what point did baptism enter the Bible? Do Jews practice baptism today? What is the meaning of Jewish baptism? Why might that be important in terms of a Christian interpretation of baptism?

3. How important is the mode of baptism?

4. Why do some denominations practice infant baptism as well as believer's baptism?

5. Why is a clear understanding of baptism necessary when we work in international or ecumenical settings? Just how tolerant are you of other people's view of baptism? Can we be too tolerant?

Activity Possibility—Reaffirming Your Baptism
Few people can verbalize the fine points of their theology related to baptism, let alone understand what other denominations believe. The following websites gives a general treatment of all major denominations.

http://www.equip.org/articles/baptism-theology/

Noted scholar J. I. Packer briefly discusses baptism in the following article.

http://www.monergism.com/thethreshold/articles/onsite/packer/baptism.html

Tanzania 2013

"The News We Prefer to Ignore"   p. 105

Discussion Theme: Persecution

1. Have you been persecuted for your faith? Persecution can involve more than physical pain. Allow group members to tell a story about being persecuted.

2. What five countries would you think actually experience the most persecution? http://www.opendoorsusa.org/persecution/about-persecution Please note that China ranks 37th. Do you think the bravery of a few people in Tiananmen Square played a role in the decline of persecution in China? Why? Why not?

3. How can one person's bravery change the course of human events? Recall a biblical character who responded with courage and consequently changed the future of a community or nation. Pick two such people and discuss their specific actions and the impact of their actions on those around them.

4. How serious would persecution have to become in order for the majority of Christians in your community to deny Christ? Remember how quickly Peter's commitment to Christ shifted to denial. (Read John 18:15-27.)

5. Bring a copy of *Fox's Book of Martyrs* to your study group and read two or three accounts of the early martyrdom of Christians. The stories are also available on line.
http://www.ccel.org/f/foxe/martyrs/fox102.htm

6. Talk about the most recent incident of Christian martyrdom you recall.

Activity Possibility—Persecution

Individuals and congregations will find the following websites informative.

Unfortunately, news agencies do not frequently report on the extensive numbers of persecutions currently occurring around the world.

http://www.persecution.org

https://www.persecution.com

U.S.A. 2013

"Opening and Closing Your Heart" p. 106

***Discussion Theme:* Deciding When to Give**

1. How generous do you consider yourself? What would you have to do to become more generous?

2. Is the Christian, trying to live by the mandates of the Bible, obligated to give to the poor? What scriptures do you find instructive in this regard?

3. "What good is it, my brothers and sisters, if someone claims to have faith but has no deeds? Can such faith save them? Suppose another person is without clothes and daily food. If one of you says to them, 'Go in peace; keep warm and well fed,' but does nothing about their physical needs, what good is it? In the same way, faith by itself, if it is not accompanied by action, is dead" (James 2:14-17). How does James link faith and action? When you hear of a person in need, what do you tend to do? Based on the counsel of James, what is the best option? What kind of need tends to tweak your desire to help others?

4. How does your church assist people who have financial needs? How is this managed?

5. What strategy do you have in regard to sharing your faith when you assist someone who has a financial need?

Activity Possibility—A Theology for Giving

The poor will always be with us. The following sites provide addition insights into the formation of a theology that takes the plight of the poor seriously.

http://www.compass1.org/the-bible-on-money/giving-to-the-poor/

http://www.zompist.com/meetthepoor.html

ABOUT THE AUTHOR

Robert and Marji Watkins have their primary residence in Sun City, Arizona. He holds degrees from Bethel University (B.S.), and Vanderbilt University (Master's of Divinity and Doctor of Ministry). He was a missionary in Colombia, South America for eight years, and served as the Director of Global Missions for the Cumberland Presbyterian Denomination for more than 20 years. He wrote *These Are My Witnesses* and has been published in more than ten periodicals, including *Decision* and *Leadership*.

Robert and Marji have five children and eight grandchildren.